Family Tree

...ev. John Brown = (1) Janet Thomson   = (2) Violet Croumbie
of Haddington   '1733'-'1771'   d. 1822
1722-178?

six children   nine children
...ho died in infancy   with descendants

Agnes Fletcher (2) = Rev. John Brown = (1) Isabella Cranston
...f seventeen children of   of Whitburn, 1754-1832
...letcher of Bridge of Teith

from this marriage descended Rev. John Brown
of Broughton Place (1784-1858) and his son
Dr John (1810-82) author of 'Rab & his Friends',
who has descendants

...and others   Janet Brown = Rev. David Smith
                     1800-1900   of Biggar
                              1792-1867

...avid Cairns = Elisabeth Williamson Smith   two sons and   Agnes Fletcher
...Stitchell   1829-1914   one daughter   1840-1935
...5-1910   d. s. p.   d. unm.

...L. Meiklejohn
...hapelknowe

...v. Principal David S. Cairns = Helen Wilson Craw, 1877-1910
   1862-1946   elder daughter of Henry Hewat Craw
                    of Foulden West Mains, Berwickshire
                    and his wife Alison Hogue

...lison Hogue Cairns   Rev. Professor David Cairns = Rosemary Russell
   1902-1959   1904-1992   1920-
   d. unm.

Elisabeth   John
1952-   1954-

ALISON CAIRNS
AND HER FAMILY

OLD CAMBUS AND THE PEASE BAY

ALISON CAIRNS AND HER FAMILY

LYN IRVINE

MONOLOGUE BOOKS

FOREWORD

EVERYONE who had known Alison Cairns accepted without surprise the suggestion that a memoir should be written and some of her letters published. The rest asked "What did she do? Why was she famous? Why do you want to write her life?" Whatever I replied they looked unconvinced, and eventually I stopped trying to justify myself. Witold Langrod, who did know her, said that he hated the idea that a book about Alison might come into the hands of people who had never been "penetrated by a sort of communion that those who knew and loved her felt in their contacts with her."

What would Alison herself think? She would be amazed at being chosen as the subject of a serious biography, but not shocked that a friend should do it in the manner of a friend. Her distinguished great-uncle had written a book about John Brown of Broughton Place, Edinburgh, his cousin by marriage, and John Brown M.D. supplied the well-known postscript to this, the *Letter to Dr John Cairns*, a Victorian masterpiece, filial and tender. A. R. MacEwen wrote his immense life of Dr John Cairns, and John Cairns the nephew, his admirable short one. And in due course Alison's father, David Smith Cairns, returned the compliment by writing the life of MacEwen, and finally he wrote his own autobiography.* It was the fashion to write and be written about within that circle of friends and relations. Both John Brown M.D. and D. S. Cairns took the risk of being misunderstood by some readers for the sake of speaking to the hearts of others, a risk that I have taken on many of these pages.

I am deeply grateful to all the friends and relatives of Alison who have helped me in many different ways. Without their support I could not have brought the book to completion. I am

* *David Cairns An Autobiography*, Edited by his Son and Daughter. S.C.M. Press Ltd 1950

v

glad to have done it, for I do believe that her story and these letters provide singular evidence of the human dilemma in the first half of this century. Among the many to whom I owe thanks Nancy Blackburn, David Cairns and Bess Tapper not only lent me much material, but read the manuscript at different stages with wonderful patience, and when my courage ebbed, implored me to exert myself, rather as the sparrows did Peter Rabbit. My sister Elsa Irvine kindly typed one of the earliest and longest versions, and later received without a murmur the information that her work was revised beyond use. I shall always remember gratefully how Carol Russell came and sat with me the day before the final version went to press and read it through with unflagging concentration. I consulted Mr J. F. Burnet of Magdalene College on the pros and cons of myself becoming a publisher for this and future books and I am particularly grateful for his help and encouragement. As for the Dickens, Bruce and Molly, I do not know where I should have been without them.

November 1966   *Lyn Irvine*
                                                            Comberton
                                                            Cambridge

vi

ILLUSTRATIONS

FOR MANY generations the paternal ancestors of Alison Cairns were shepherds and farm-labourers on the Scottish Border, a hard-pressed and obscure family without prospect of any other way of living. But in the first half of the nineteenth century the mould was broken by the appearance among them of a child prodigy; this was John Cairns (1818–92) who grew up to be a man of spectacular parts, one of the first scholars of his time. Nothing daunted him. He possessed the sanguine outlook that often goes with health and a powerful frame, and could talk hopefully of the devil losing ground and of Waterloo as the world's last great battlefield. Some of this confidence was passed on to his brother David, with whom he shared his success. His great-niece Alison, the subject of this book, responded to the mood of her home with such spirits that her grandmother called her a bird of joy.

She was born in 1902 in the United Presbyterian Manse at Ayton, a village six miles from Berwick-upon-Tweed, in that unspoilt lozenge of land, the county of Berwick. To live there is almost to live on an island, for the sea flanks it on the north-east, the Tweed on the south and west, while the empty uplands of the Lammermoors fill all the northern part of the county. The soft falling line of the moors breaks suddenly away in the wall of sea-cliffs, three hundred feet high at St Abb's Head and five hundred above Fast Castle. Where the burns scooped a passage down to the sea the resolute fisherfolk built their homes at the water's edge, but for the greater part of its twenty miles, the coast of Berwickshire belongs to the fulmars, the cormorants, shags and peregrines, foxes and otters. Birds and beasts which centuries ago entered legend and history with local lords or holy men outlive here in their generations the churches and families which once overshadowed them.

The Lammermoors, once true mountains, were levelled by folding and erosion at some long distant time. Yet the horizons here are so featureless that they give the impression of youth rather than age. As the rain clouds peel up, the firmament above and the land below seem newly divorced in the pageant of creation. South of the Lammermoors lies the wealth of the county, in the plain sloping down to the Tweed and watered by its tributaries, where seagulls follow the tractor over wide chocolate-coloured fields capped with groves of oak and beech. The Merse, as they call this part of Berwickshire, is a huge saucer of land tilting gently towards the sea, yet not tilting so much that the pristine river or its parent glacier could spill out easily, as it swerved east and north, swung off-course by the formidable obstacle of the Cheviot. So the Tweed, as it approached the North Sea, dug the channel which adds so much to the beauty and the character of this stretch of the Borders, and in other centuries so increased the problems of the warring nations.

Since 1482 the county has perforce worn its heart upon the cuff of Northumberland, and that heart is Berwick-upon-Tweed, built upon the slopes of the last loop of the river, and once dominated by the great castle. The railway station stands where from 1306 to 1310 the Countess of Buchan was caged like a wild beast for placing the crown of Scotland on the head of Robert the Bruce, and the Royal Border Bridge, Stephenson's noble viaduct on its twenty-seven giant stems, now lays the land open to the southerner. When the railway line leaves the town it follows the cliff-edge as far as Burnmouth, and after hundreds of miles of sober English country the bold Berwickshire coast flashes past the carriage windows: sea and sky and coiling birds, red rocks over the lip of the meadows, and the burrows of bygone smugglers. Then avoiding the deep cleft where the Burn dives down to its mouth, both rail and road turn sharply inland, following first the Eye Water (on which Ayton stands) and then the Pease Burn.

This is all Cairns country, but for the earliest known ancestors of Alison on her father's side we must go west to the Lammermoors themselves and to the very heart of the moors, where below a strange cairn called the Deil's Mitten, marking, they say, the burial place of a Pictish king, lies the farm of Byrecleugh, not far from the head of the Dye Water and four or five miles from the high road through Longformacus. In this desolate place a Thomas Cairns was tenant farmer at the beginning of the eighteenth century. He had nine daughters but only one son, Thomas, born in 1750, who became a wandering shepherd and was buried in the graveyard of the old church at Bonkyl in 1799, near the ruins of Bonkyl Castle, once a Stewart residence. Forty-nine years is a short life, but of them forty may have been strenuously spent, and until well on in the nineteenth century the animals on Berwickshire farms were almost as well housed as the workers, and not more cramped. In cottages twelve foot square families of ten or twelve slept and ate together, and the children played or learned their lessons while the father cobbled and the mother spun thread from the flax she had grown. Even for the crises of life there was no other shelter – here they were conceived and born, endured any illness that came, and here they died. And "they were contented with their situation" as it says in the *New Statistical Account of Scotland*. Were they still digesting the blessing of peace which came to the Borders after so many centuries of tribulation? (The only manual skill of John Cairns as a boy was making *ousels*, the iron tips for arrows.) They carried the trials of their forebears about their hearts, unlike those who learn history from books, and lived almost as close to the earth as sheep in the struggle to wring a living from it, knowing the relish of surviving each day by each day's labour. A hind's (labourer's) privileges were "House and yard; coals driven; cow's grass in summer and fodder in winter; ten bolls of oats or oatmeal; ten firlots of barley; four to six firlots of pease; 1000–1500 yards of potato-drill; a peck's sowing of lint or £1 in lieu; £3 to £4 of money."*

The wild and lonely countryside encouraged the spirit of endurance, and even the lake-like beauty of the lower reaches of the Tweed, deceptively sensuous and secure, did not bring wealth to the people, since water which fell so gradually was

* *New Statistical Account of Scotland.* Edinburgh 1845. Rev. John Gifford on Nenthorn, Berwickshire.

3

poor in sites for mills. Other Border counties captured the weaving industry, and Berwickshire remained almost entirely dependent upon agriculture and sheep-farming.

The early generations of the Cairns family rarely stayed long in the same cottage under the same farmer; it was the custom at the hiring fair on May 12 each year for the labour force of Berwickshire to be reshuffled like a pack of cards. Then the farmer sent a couple of long carts to collect his new hind, and on these the furniture and possessions were stacked – sometimes even the grate and the windows – and on top of the goods went the family, old and young, in whatever state of health the day might find them. A migration like this brought one of the sons of Thomas the shepherd of Bonkyl to the extreme north-east of the county and the windswept plateau of Oldcambus – wooded in Bruce's time, for he pitched his camp in Oldcambus wood. It was a bleak place, but stimulating. The ruined church near the cliffs had been dedicated to St Helena the mother of Constantine the Great by three Northumbrian princesses of the seventh century. The fresh coastline to Tantallon and the Firth of Forth unrolled like a great chart to the north, and Edinburgh was within walking distance, only thirty-four miles by road through Haddington. Two years later the family were living in the forester's cottage in the Pease Dean, the fine wooded glade inland from Oldcambus, known to Cromwell as "the strait pass at Copperspath" where his army was held by General Leslie before the battle of Dunbar. Copperspath is Cockburnspath, a village of character and great age, and here the Cairns children went to school under an able dominie called MacGregor, who picked out the third child, John, as a pupil deserving his special attention. Since the next move took them no further afield than Dunglass, just north of the village, the children had the rare advantage of MacGregor's continued care. John left school at thirteen to help his father with the sheep on the Dunglass estate, but his mother contrived to meet the cost of his going to Mac-Gregor in the evenings to prepare for the university. While he watched the sheep he could shelter in another ruin, finer than St Helen's, the collegiate church of Dunglass, and take his book from his plaidneuk.

4

His schoolfellows regarded him as a "raill dungeon o' wut," meaning he was very profound – the phrase was used of Dr Johnson by Lady Lochbuy. But over and above this "wut" were industry and resolution. A fellow student bowling through the night in the stage coach to Edinburgh, caught sight at Haddington of John Cairns walking by the cart of the Cockburnspath carrier, on his way to the university for the first time, and noted the expression on the young man's face, keen and purposeful to no ordinary degree. None of his family had ever possessed leisure or consorted with those who did, and so he set himself to study with all the energy that a farm labourer might need to keep alive, and gave as many hours to his books as a shepherd to his flocks in the lambing season. There comes a day when the last lamb has been born or the last turnip lifted from the field, but in the new calling among words and symbols and ideas, there was no limit to what might be achieved. John's ability was admired by all and became a source of wonder to the man himself. "I could never have believed that I could have driven so much thought through my head in a single day as I have sometimes been obliged to do."

He had been brought up in the devout and strict tradition of a branch of the Presbyterian Secession Church – the Burghers – with Church and Sunday School, Bible reading and Family Prayers and the Shorter Catechism integral parts of life, but in his first years as a student he became critical of the "pious cant of the godly" and discussed with his friends the danger that belief might "suspend or destroy the exercise of the intellectual powers." "I abominate," he wrote to a cousin, "confessions and recitals of religious experience." After the first year at Edinburgh he left the university for lack of money and taught for two years at Ayton, and then returned to complete his course with even greater success. He supported himself largely by private teaching and saved enough for a winter of studies in Berlin and a grand tour of Europe – mainly on foot. To all his professors he appeared marked out for an academic career of great distinction, but inner currents of which we have no record were moving differently, and after six years of prodigious study, he gave up the life of the university and entered the Secession Church,

5

becoming in 1845 the minister of Golden Square Church in Berwick-upon-Tweed.

By our standards to-day, he was a dull preacher, with a delivery that shocked even his mother – "oor John aye wampishing wi' his airms" – but he knew how to serve and comfort the people of his congregation. Long afterwards someone questioned an old woman in Berwick about his preaching. "Ay, I suppose he was a fine preacher. But I *know* he was my kind dear friend." The absurdity of standing up there in the pulpit, holding forth, a big man in a black gown and black gloves, this had been almost his undoing when he saw through the window, in splendid contrast, a hen with her chicks foraging in the dust. He was famed and remembered for the heartiness of his laugh.

After John Cairns had been two years in Berwick, his congregation raised his stipend by £20, giving him the longed-for means to help his brother David, still in field and forest work at Dunglass. On this £20 David was able to return to study with MacGregor, and after a few months he was ready to enter Edinburgh University. This brotherly act changed everything for him and his descendants. Ten years later David also was ordained in the church and became minister at Stitchel near Kelso, marrying the following year Elisabeth Smith, daughter of the Reverend David Smith of Biggar, and of his wife Janet Brown (1800–1900), grand-daughter of the Reverend John Brown of Haddington, one of the outstanding figures in the history of the Scottish church. John himself did not marry. When a new manse was built, 3 Wellington Terrace, on the walls of Berwick, his sister Janet came to look after him and the house, so that he could maintain the extraordinary frugality with time for which he was renowned. No records of Janet's gifts or interests, or even of her character survive. A. R. MacEwen in his long life of John Cairns never calls her from below stairs. Probably he did not see that she mattered, although John's whole career would have foundered but for her ministrations. Fifty years she gave to protecting him from thinking or doing anything about the mere business of living and its attendant problems. If I labour an old familiar grievance it is because its shadow lies right across the story to come.

At the manse John chose as his study a room on the first floor which had two windows, one looking west over the Tweed, the other south to the open sea and Lindisfarne and Bamborough, both places of ancient, holy memory. At the south window he always sat to work, as my father himself did in later years when he also became minister to the same congregation.*

Until the middle seventies of the century three of the Cairns brothers, strategically placed, continued to set the mark of their natures upon Berwickshire, for besides John at Berwick and David at Stitchel, there was William the schoolmaster at Oldcambus, deeply loved, and remembered there to this day. William had begun life as a stonemason, but fell seriously ill after standing long hours in the Whiteadder building the bridge at Allanton, and lost the use of both legs. He taught his pupils from a massive wheel-chair, and made his journeys by trap driving a black pony called Bismarck. When this delightful man, with his bland, whiskered, bespectacled face, set off to visit the family at Stitchel, it became a "triumphal progress" from one farmhouse to the next. There was hardly a parish in the whole county without some relative or welcoming friend, and when many years later one of this line returned to visit places known in childhood, his look and carriage spoke for him and the man came from the byre saying "I ken fine ye're a Cairns."

Most of the questions we long to ask never entered the minds of John Cairns' contemporaries and biographers. And when he met William Wordsworth and considered it one of the high moments of his life, they exchanged polite banalities. But by picking out the rare human detail from MacEwen's classical life we can see that the pattern was far more intricate than he suspected – or wished to admit. For one thing, the strain of so arduous and unnatural a routine brought on a nervous breakdown, sleeplessness, loss of memory, even mental sluggishness. MacEwen merely says "His health broke down completely." His doctor† ordered a complete change, and several times in

* When a new church was built in 1859, Golden Square became Wallace Green
† This was Dr Philip Maclagan, son-in-law of Dr George Johnston, physician and naturalist, and the first of the three great Maclagan doctors who succoured their patients in Berwick for more than a century

his thirties he was obliged to travel abroad in search of renewal. His most ambitious project, a book on the difficulties of the Christian faith, never took shape – it was itself too difficult – and soon "the whole process of book-production," so he said, became "distasteful." Christianity impressed him much more as lived than as propounded, and sermons he believed would go out of fashion – in the millennium which he hoped was shortly to begin.

All this time his brother clergy and distinguished laymen of the church were nagging him to leave Berwick and take more important and influential work. Even the peculiar honour of becoming principal of Edinburgh University was offered, and refused so quietly that his own family knew nothing of it until he died. The very stones of Berwick were dear to him, he said, and Stitchel drew him as it drew William. His nephew David remembered him coming in from the garden and seeking out his sister-in-law. "I have come to tell you that this is a day that has wandered out of Paradise." That was how they talked, in deep rich voices, with just a trace of self-mockery.* And sometimes with gentle mockery of others – as when John mentioned the prayers put up in Golden Square, forty years before his time, for the "fall of the Bloody House of Bourbon." "France does not know how much she is indebted to the prayers of those good people."

He was a most gifted linguist and his interest in languages never waned. He learned a new one as readily as most men take a holiday, in fact a few hours rubbing up his Dutch or his Danish or his Assyrian was his favourite relaxation. In his old age he learned Arabic, gratified to be able to pray for the conversion of the Muslims in the language of their prophet. In 1876 he was persuaded to leave Berwick for Edinburgh to become joint professor of Systematic Theology and Apologetics at the Theological Hall of the United Presbyterian Church, and three years later he became principal of the Hall. Janet was still with him and they lived at 10 Spence Street, off the Dalkeith Road, where William joined them to occupy himself in retirement by

---

* Tom Taylor, late Principal of Aberdeen University, could reproduce this voice admirably, quoting D. S. Cairns – "Tom, the Larig is the Gateway to Eternity"

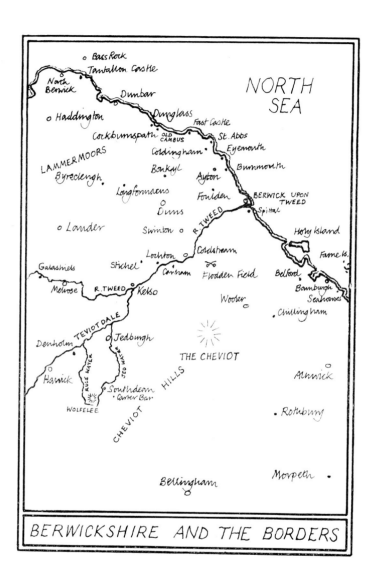

BERWICKSHIRE AND THE BORDERS

making an index of the eleventh edition of the Encyclopaedia Britannica. So they spent the last decades of their lives, observing still many of the habits formed in the shepherd's cottage at Dunglass – the family prayers, the bowl of porridge for supper – and "standing like a wall" behind the young nephews from Stitchel when they came to Edinburgh to study.

John Cairns died after a short illness in 1892, mourned and venerated, but how widely venerated no one knew until the day of his funeral when the great hall of the United Presbyterian College was crowded, and thousands more followed in the procession and lined the streets of Edinburgh, as though a prince had passed away, a national hero.

John's brother David had been much helped in the education of his three sons by a little fortune of £500 left him by Thomas Wilson of Haymount, in gratitude for the minister's prayers and visits during a long illness. The two families were drawn together. Mr Wilson's niece was the wife of Henry Hewat Craw of Foulden West Mains, a successful and benevolent farmer, and the young Cairns visited Foulden, played with the little Craw children, took them for walks and told them stories, and – as one of the children recollected eighty years later – rode the ponies round the fields "rather *hard*, my dear." This Henry Craw was also a notable naturalist and authority on Border matters. His ancestors were all people of metal and ability, and his grandfather, James, born in 1747, showed the stuff he was made of at the age of six by refusing to return to school after the master had punished him. He never did return, but educated himself "by his own industry and a little assistance from others," as his son put on record. He thus became a man of wide reading, mastering with such success the contents of a library of law books left to him by an uncle that all his neighbours came to him for legal advice. In 1810 he gave over the management of his farm, Lauder West Mains, to his eldest son, also James, and only sixteen at the time. The young man had every kind of confidence. He went up yearly to the Selkirk Tryst, and one year, returning through Edinburgh, he found the High Street in an uproar; two Lauder men had been condemned for sheep-stealing and were to be hanged the next day. James Craw rode home with all speed, knocked up the townsfolk and gave them the news. About thirty or forty young blades mounted without delay and rode to Edinburgh and breaking into the Tolbooth rescued their fellows and carried them home. For the sake of safety however the condemned men left Lauder and settled in another part of Berwickshire – Swinton, some twenty miles away – and there they did very well and lived to a ripe age.

Henry Hewat Craw was this James's younger son, and his boyhood had been sad, for his mother died after only eight years of married life, and his two sisters developed tuberculosis at a boarding school in Melrose and both died in their teens. When Henry's own cherished daughters, Helen and Barbara, were ready for school, he took a house in Edinburgh and lodged them there like two royal princesses, with a governess in residence (although they attended St Margaret's School) and the usual staff of those days. Helen was serious and intellectual and grew with the years from being child-companion to being equal and friend of one of the young people from the Stitchel Manse, the third of that family, "Mr David" as she called him, writing him lively letters in her strong Hanoverian hand. The first of these was written from Rawburn, the shepherd's cottage in the Lammermoors, where the young Craws spent their holidays, entertaining their friends, riding, *grumping* for trout in the burns, or lying in the heather reading. Helen spoke of the subdued skies and gleams of sunshine which are among the special charms of that Border country. They seemed to her to "harmonize with these great long moors."

David Smith Cairns had been born in 1862, and Helen Craw in 1876, but owing to the vicissitudes of his twenties and thirties, David was still unmarried by 1900. His story is full of contrasts to his uncle John's: the boyhood with pony-riding at Foulden and trout-fishing in the Eden, and the occasion of a wonderful flight of mockery when he broke down reciting Schiller at a school prize-giving and filled in the gaps with gibberish. Although he recalled this with horror, it stamps him as the original he always remained, untrammelled by respect for the insignificant. Little went easily for him at first. He achieved an ordinary Master of Arts degree at Edinburgh after a long struggle. He lost his faith entirely for a time and his health broke down, and only after a winter in Egypt were both health and faith restored enough for him to carry on in the family tradition and enter the Theological Hall. Even after that, as a probationer of the church, he suffered many disappointments, preaching in fifteen or sixteen vacancies without finding acceptance. In 1895, at the age of thirty-two, he was called to Ayton, a place full of family associations and only five miles across the fields from Foulden.*

* After the death of Thomas Cairns, the Bonkyl shepherd, his widow Janet and her five children went to an empty farmhouse on the top of Ayton Hill, Janet to be henwife and swineherd, and the elder son James to be shepherd

THREE years later, in 1898, my father was called from Liverpool to Wallace Green Church in Berwick – the church which replaced Golden Square forty years earlier in Dr John Cairns' time. He was soon drawn into the cordial circle of the Cairns and the Craws. The laconic entries in his pocket diaries burgeoned when he went to tea with Mrs Craw at Foulden to "Tea on the lawn" or "Tea in the garden," and by this expansiveness I know it must have been a particular pleasure. The entry would bring back to him the view of England across the Tweed, England – however deceptively – looking like Beulah's Land, with the Cheviot as the Delectable Mountains, soft-coloured, withdrawn, yet visible over an immense area of the Borders and far out to sea, where the first Christian missionaries lifted up their eyes to that noble outline and the sleek grass pelt, as sensitive as water to the changing sky.

The friendship between D. S. Cairns and Helen Craw had grown steadily closer, and they were married on 3 December 1901, to change the pattern of coming and going between Ayton and Foulden, but not change it greatly, and Barbara frequently rode over to her sister on horseback unless their mother could persuade her to take the trap and carry gifts from the farm and garden. On the afternoon of 12 March 1902, I know from my father's diary that the Cairns called at Wallace Green Manse, and if we were all at home that day, they were entertained by my parents and five children under ten. Perhaps they came with an invitation, for on April 28 – an unprecedented event – my mother went away though only for one night. She stayed with the Cairns at Ayton, and returned there again in September, and on October 18 the Cairns' first child was born and christened Alison Hogue, after her maternal grandmother.

When I first saw D. S. Cairns I have no idea. He must have

peered at me in my cradle, and his countenance was im-
memorially familiar to me. The precocity of infants was a
matter of great interest to him, and Alison seems to have been
livelier and more precocious than average, although she vexed
me beyond measure at our first meeting at the manse in Berwick
by crushing to bits the miniature doll's cradle, made of an
eggshell, which I had laid with a warning in her outstretched
hand. We were both ignorant – I of babies, she of eggshells – for
I was still under three and Alison not much over a year. She
was propped on the sofa in our dining-room with her black
boots hardly reaching to the frame of the seat, while her mother
sat beside her, holding a glass of milk, which the little thing
required some coaxing to take. On this visit, Alison's mother
and mine again had confidences to exchange, for both were
expecting a child that summer, and they were now on first-name
terms which in those days was a slow and difficult achievement.
(My father and D. S. Cairns remained Irvine and Cairns to one
another for the whole remainder of their very long lives.) David
was born, the Cairns' second and last child, on 11 June 1904.

Alison's clearest and earliest memories were of Foulden and
not Ayton. She remembered an evening service held in the
kitchen of the farmhouse, with planks laid across chairs to
squeeze in all the hinds and their families. Her father was
preaching and it was something quite new to sit up so late.
"Very loud singing and lamplight. I think that Grannie was
carried down for it, anyhow it was all rather solemn and
enjoyable." Again to hear their father preach they were driven
from Foulden to a village beyond their usual ambit, and Uncle
James Craw pointed out cross-roads on the boundary between
England and Scotland, and a hill where witches had been
burned. Already deeply excited, Alison gazed at her father in
the pulpit until her fatigued eyes saw a blue haze round his
head, which she knew to be a sign that he was a very good man.
Would it save him from a *faux pas*, however? He might do
something improper – might be sick in the pulpit. Indeed once
he rather shocked the congregation by announcing the hymn
with a shout – HOLY, HOLY, HOLY. But for David it was a
moment of rapture.

In the winter of 1906–7 the fair prospects of the family at Ayton received a tragic blow. Helen Cairns developed the first signs of Bright's Disease, and in the fashion of an earlier time the incurable nature of the illness was broken to her without delay. She bore it with great fortitude. It was all the harder since in 1907, at forty-four – an age when his uncle John had burned his genius almost to the socket – D. S. Cairns was only at the beginning of his true career. His courage and originality as a theologian had been observed and by itself would have carried him a long way, but there was so much more – his spontaneous interest in people, and a sense of humour like a skeleton key to every situation; the voice with its wonderful depth and timbre, and the noble presence in which the lineaments of the frail young man could scarcely be traced. This unwanted probationer of the nineties was elected in 1907 into the chair of Dogmatics and Apologetics at the United Free Church College in Aberdeen.

When their rented house, 10 Rubislaw Terrace, was in order, the invalid Helen travelled north with the two children. David, a sober little boy of three, not vivacious like Alison – the one who "needed to be checked" according to her aunt Barbara – sat on his mother's knee in the dining-room of their new home and presently drew her attention to the fact that They had the same pictures as Us. The two children have the look of little exiles as they were photographed standing by the front door of the new home, shy, unsmiling, wearing wide-brimmed sailor hats beribboned with "H.M.S. Berwick."

The following year my father was called to the South United Free Church in Aberdeen and we moved in the spring of 1908 to the manse in Westfield Terrace, no distance from either Rubislaw Terrace or Hamilton Place – to which the Cairns moved in 1910. When we were taken to see Helen Cairns she was resting on the sofa in the study, with a white cashmere shawl draped over her head and shoulders. Her manner of greeting and speaking was like a benediction, and her

> unblinded eyes
> Saw far and near the fields of Paradise.

14

On this same sofa, supported in her husband's arms and listening to his prayers, she presently died, after as brief a married life as her grandmother, only eight years. Before she left the children, she had taught them to say the Forty-second Psalm, looking far into their future when she made the strange choice.

I was old enough to be terrified of losing my own mother, but not old enough to pity Alison, who hid her confusion by bragging in the kitchen about the role she would play as a step-daughter if her father married again. The fact that those who die are not there any more was impossible to accept for a long time, but at last in her little bedroom in Hamilton Place, between sleep and sleep, she understood it "with the sharpness of revelation." Too young to take this revelation to herself and still too wounded to relate it to her mother, she thought of her beloved Highland aunts* as doomed to vanish on the flood. "All their richness of memory and their youth in the far north being swept away, it cut me to the very heart." Again in the night she woke to see her own hand lie strangely on the sheet, its familiarity gone, her title to that flesh and blood in doubt, and the mystery of its provenance in space and time ousting everything else.

The essential nature of people whom we love in childhood becomes part of everything most pervasive and least definite in the world around us. So Alison and David found in the obscure times which followed their mother's death. A cousin of friends looked after them, and was "simply a dragon," an anxious little spinster of forty, with no experience of small children. Alison and David drew closer to one another for self-protection and lived for the visits to Berwickshire – for the warmth and indulgence of family gatherings in surroundings where scents and sounds and even the quality of the light beguiled them into hoping that the past could come again. Perhaps it was this hope that made the enchantment of Christmas at Lochton with Aunt Barbara and Uncle Jo† so impossible to explain to anyone, a private, exquisite happiness that broke into blossom as the bells of Carham across the Tweed rang out midnight on the

---

* Christina and Elspeth Cumming, see p. 20

† In 1903 Barbara Craw had married John Aitchison, farmer, of Lochton, between Coldstream and Kelso

twenty-fourth. "It had no relation whatever to any experience other than itself." Kelso was their town, one of their "native places," where Alison and David knew all the people in the shops round the elegant square, and the Tweed surged under the bridge, still "a' solid water" as when the village idiot from Stitchel viewed it from Great-uncle William's pony-trap.

When I first went to Mr Mackie's School in Aberdeen, Alison and David were at Miss Knowles', but Alison presently came to Mr Mackie's too, and delighted the school inspector, Dr Wattie, with her example of euphemism. "You could say that a man was fond of the bottle." When Margaret Thirde became our headmistress and produced *The Land of Heart's Desire*, Alison was cast as Father Hart. She was only thirteen, but when she stood in front of the stage speaking the last lines of the play, she looked like a figure from a Byzantine mosaic. The well-known verse has worn to the texture of tissue paper; Alison's gravity outlasts for me both the legend and the part – and she herself thought Yeats' twilight contrived even then. She brought me two books of her father's which were more to her taste – Edith Sichel's *Women and Men of the French Renaissance* and *Catherine de' Medici and the French Reformation*. We studied the faint but exquisite illustrations, Clouet and *d'après* Clouet, and discussed the owners of these faces, the clever passionate women with Alison's arched eyebrows and high rounded forehead. These were her people. While the rest of us were still taken up with our class-mates, D. S. Cairns' always enlarging circle had begun to interest her. She was pleased to go up on the platform after a meeting to shake hands with a plain stocky Russian woman, Tolstoy's daughter Alexandra; and already before the war Pastor Le Seur (who afterwards consoled and advised Edith Cavell in prison) was a visitor at Hamilton Place. Alison was proud of her father's position for the glory of it, but D. S. Cairns did not look at it that way. Common tastes and interests and nothing else led him to find or be found by Neville Talbot and the Motts, Baron von Hügel, Reinhold Niebuhr, the Masaryks and many more.

Alison lent me the Sichel books long enough for the portraits to stay imprinted on my memory, but before I could read the text, my father did, and was alarmed for my innocence, and requested me to return the books to Alison at once. "I suppose it's because she says that kings had mistresses." We were walking along Westfield Terrace away from the manse as she said this. There had been a moment by lamplight at Christmas when David first consciously looked at his sister's face. Now I too had my moment of awareness. Now I also could see how brilliant her grey eyes were and how thick the straight eyelashes. Her nose was strong, too strong for perfect beauty, but the mouth was small and full in an oval face with gentle contours. She took after her mother and the Craws, but also had her likeness many generations earlier on her father's side, in Ebenezer Brown of Inverkeithing, himself often likened to Erasmus; and the death mask of Mary Queen of Scots* – whose ancestors also lived at Bonkyl – might almost be Alison's.

During our schooldays in Aberdeen I was a little intimidated by Alison and David. David studied astronomy and dared me to name any crater on the moon, and his confidence in my ignorance made me think that Copernicus must be wrong, or at least I would pronounce it wrongly, so I held my tongue and writhed. Whereupon Alison produced a mahogany planchette on which we flattened our small palms and hoped for a message from The Beyond. But this unchildish toy merely covered the paper with chicken-tracks. Their knowledge of French was humbling too. They had acquired it from a tiny and charming Parisian governess who lived with them for a year, and leaning towards a revival of the Auld Alliance, Alison began to use tags of French and never lost the habit; and she now gave her devotion to Mary Queen of Scots for good and all, although she knew nothing of her physical and more than physical resemblance to this queen.

In those days children did a great deal of blushing for the ignorance of some things and the awareness of other things, but Alison, although she blushed too, had considerable self-possession. She sat down readily at our piano and played me a little piece of descriptive music inspired by the *vendanges*, and as her fingers rattled over the keys she turned her head quickly saying

* This is now at Lennoxlove

17

"Now the peasants are dancing down between the rows of vines." It was the first and last time that I heard her play any musical instrument. When she was eleven or twelve, she had her first experience of a long time in bed. Bicycling in the roads above Kings Gate with the Forgan girls and Betty Duncan, she had overbalanced, fallen in a tangle with the machine and broken her leg between knee and ankle. Jessie Cairns, her father's sister was in charge at the time, and told me that it had been a bad moment when the doctor set the fractured bone. She lay for a long time in a little ground-floor room at 62 Hamilton Place with a cage over her legs and afterwards there was a slight unevenness in her walk, specially when she hurried. She looked all her life as if her shoe pinched.

In 1916 D. S. Cairns was invited to lecture to the troops in France under the auspices of the Y.M.C.A., and before he left the country, fearing a long separation from his children (now aged thirteen and eleven) he felt compelled to write instructing them how they should live. Always an expansive letter-writer – he had once written A. G. Hogg one hundred and twelve pages – he sent them ten quarto pages now, and it is evident from the thumbed and dog-eared condition of the manuscript that Alison and David realized how deeply important it was. He urged them to pray, to read their Bibles and observe the Sabbath. Looking forward, knowing that he would be very near the front line and might never return to these motherless children, he warned them against strong drink and bad company. He could not foresee how quickly and radically his own evangelism was about to change, not in content but in manner. The letter was probably his last tribute to the religious outlook of the nineteenth century. When the war ended and he finished drafting the report of the findings of the committee on the Army and Religion, he was in close touch not only with other communions but with a much younger generation than his own. From 1919 onwards he never stood still, but in 1916, when he wrote to the children, he had forgotten in his intense anxiety how little the preaching of his father and his uncle John attracted him in his youth, forgotten also Uncle John's own frank distaste for the pious talk of *his* elders. Alison was no less critical than they had been. If she spread out a spiritual tentacle, it was only for a moment, before folding up in a huff at the impropriety of it all. I observed with interest and surprise how at family prayers she scuffed the polished floor with the legs of the chair at which she knelt, hoping to break the thread of her father's invocations when he lost sense of time. Only one conclusion could be drawn from that letter, or even from my parents' teaching, which by the time they got to their sixth child was very light in touch, a matter of little stories, tactfully chosen object lessons; the conclusion that man's chief end is to be good, and goodness consists in pleasing one's elders and betters. But we had also the Shorter Catechism, the words the children in the Dunglass cottage repeated every Sunday night, the words all Scottish children had been learning for centuries, suggested by Calvin himself. Q. *What is man's chief end?* A. *Man's chief end is to glorify God and enjoy him for ever.* How that startled me! I read it over and over again, marvelling at the heart-lifting contradiction of all I had hitherto supposed to be man's chief end. But no one else looked pleased. My Sunday School teacher remained grave. No one mentioned it. So there followed sadly a suspension of belief.

On the departure of D. S. Cairns for France, the house in Hamilton Place was sublet and Alison and David went to live in Edinburgh with their Aunt Jaye, Jessie Cairns, at 20 Braidburn Crescent. Here the Cairns grandparents (now both dead) had retired from the manse at Stitchel in 1900. It was a dark house, loaded with old family stuff, including the wheel-chair in which Great-uncle William had spent so much of his life. Jessie Cairns preferred reading books and writing letters to housekeeping, but like all the other unmarried women preceding her in that family, she accepted without protest the tasks of looking after people and houses and even children when the need arose. She was tall and plain and angular, usually rather drably dressed, and she *looked* unmarried, as the good spinster women did in those days; but I have never forgotten the humorous, deprecating – almost sardonic – expression of her mouth when she laughed, and the unvarying kindness of her eyes.

William Cairns, D. S. Cairns' younger brother, was minister

of Davidson Church, Eyre Place, Edinburgh, and lived at 82 Howard Place with his wife Christina (aunt Kirsty) one of the remarkable daughters of the Reverend James Cumming, minister at Melness from 1861 until his death more than forty years later. Millicent, Duchess of Sutherland, who founded the Highland Home Industries, took Kirsty as a girl to be her secretary and aide, and together they had travelled all over the north by land and sea.* This aunt, herself childless, was much loved by Alison and David. They used to spend their Sundays at Howard Place, going to hear the uncle preach in the evenings, listening when they returned to the aunt's stories of her childhood in Melness, a place so remote, fifty miles from Lairg over rough and exposed roads, that life there still retained some of the roughness and simplicity and also the nobleness of primitive times. Like Alison, Aunt Kirsty had broken her leg as a girl, but in a more dramatic way altogether. She was in her father's gig, which was being driven to Melness from Tongue by a "coorse young lad." He took the turn at the bridge over the burn too fast; the wheel caught the parapet on the seaward side of the bridge, and Kirsty was thrown out and over the bridge into a pool. The mark of the wheel on the stone was visible for many years, reminding the parishioners of the accident, though indeed in those parts little is ever forgotten.

In Edinburgh David went to Merchiston Castle School and Alison to St George's, but in September 1918 she was sent as a boarder to the Mount, the Quaker School in York, and felt the promise of happiness the moment she stepped over the threshold. And at the Mount the first conception of tolerance came to her under the discreet guidance of the Friends. To warm to the congenial was not enough, and she began to consider also the uncongenial; the odd, the plain, the stupid; and realized that by nature she was very hard to please.

Her bounding spirits show on every page of her diary for

---

* In 1955 David, visiting Melness for the first time, met an old crofter who had been at school with his aunts. "The last time I saw Miss Teenie she was coming along the road with quite a group of people, and she left them and came up to my garden wall and said 'Donald, will you come over here?' I came over and saw the lady she was with and said 'If I am not mistaken, is this not Millicent the Duchess of Sutherland herself?' And she said 'Yes I am,' and spoke with me very pleasantly for some time."

1919, in which she even recorded the progress of an attack of measles up to a temperature of 104·6, with singular almost scientific detachment and without a trace of homesickness. She had not known the indulgence for which a sick child away at school might crave, and she was on the whole well and very gay. This time at the Mount bears no resemblance to the three years at Mr Mackie's school, on the contrary – "never was so sore with laughing in my life" – that wonderful laugh as sudden as a river in spate bursting its banks, as natural and impossible to control. The muscles of her face and sides ached and she almost fell off the walls of York, she laughed so hard. Scripture gave some trouble – "all of a muddle of Isaiah and Jeremiah" – so did mathematics – "ghastly and hopeless geometry" – but she applied herself eagerly to English Literature, and to History and French, and in the summer of 1919 was rewarded by a telegram from Miss Sturge, the headmistress. "I opened it with a sinking heart but it said 'Passed with honours splendid.' " Girton College accepted her for the Michaelmas Term of 1921 and she left the Mount at Christmas 1920, grateful, melancholy, caught again by the magic of the festival when seniors and leavers went round the school before dawn with candles and flashlights singing "Christians awake."

D. S. Cairns had returned to Aberdeen and Alison now joined him there, to live "rather drearily" in lodgings and take her solitary constitutionals. Walking by Byron's Cottage, that magnet of our childhood, she found again the scilla in the rough grass. We imagined that it survived from the time when the shabby little stone house was improbably inhabited by the most sensational of all English poets. Alison had been reading *A Winter's Tale* – "and a first visit abroad was in prospect and then Cambridge and launching into life, it seemed, and I felt quite intoxicated and everything went to the rhythm of 'daffodils that come before the swallow dares and take the winds of March with beauty.' " How soon these expectations were fulfilled, I know from a cherished picture postcard which she sent me from Paris in July. On the one side, the Victory of Samothrace, on the other she had written "Lyn, I can't believe I'm me! Adventures have simply crowded on me thick and fast this last fortnight." She had been staying with a Protestant pastor and his wife in Nantes, a M. and Mme Cremer. When she arrived at the presbytery towards the end of May she found a swarm of little Cremers and five pensionnaires – three from Scandinavia, two girls and a boy; a Scottish youth, Graham; and Francis a proud-looking and reserved Londoner.* He and Graham were both going up to Oxford in October, but that was all they had in common, apart from a distaste for Scandinavians. Francis noted in his journal that Miss Cairns seemed to be "a Scotch girl of some vigour, a complete contrast to the soft and timid Scandinavian misses." After a few days' temporizing, to make sure that she would appreciate the offer, he invited her to join him on a country walk. Alison accepted eagerly. She had never been further south than York, and the water meadows of the Loire valley amazed her. No search for the retiring scilla here; they waded in purple orchis and marguerites. Francis noticed how gamely she went through thickets and over walls and fences, and how easily she held her own in literary quotations. Here was somebody almost as saturated in poetry as he was himself. Soon Alison perceived the loneliness behind Graham's grudging manner, and contrived to bring the two young men together, and with them she entered into a flippant alliance to mystify the other pensionnaires. Graham was the grandson of a successful engineer who had started life without a penny, but like so many who are born two generations from a burst of energy and ambition, he regarded life with a certain disillusion. Francis' problem was entirely different and third generation lassitude lay far behind him. His pride, and possibly also his addiction to Malory's *Morte d'Arthur*, sprang partly from knowing that he could trace his ancestors back to the eleventh century and that *then* they were men of culture. One similarity between Francis and Alison at this time was a warm attachment to their parents. The long confiding letters which Francis sent home survive to give as limpid a version of the summer of 1921 as one could hope to recover at this date. They are not at all like the letters that boys of eighteen usually wrote to their parents even in those days,

* Graham and Francis are pseudonyms, otherwise characters in this book are given their own names

but both his parents had concerned themselves to an uncommon degree with the upbringing of their children – as D. S. Cairns had concerned himself with Alison and David.

The presbytery was large even for a presbytery and stood in a garden with a high wall over the top of which the swallows screamed and stormed, while beyond in the rue de Gigant the trams also screamed, swinging down their hot rails. In the wall was an iron door with a bell and when someone rang the bell, Madame or the *bonne à tout faire* could open it by a mechanism in the house, as garden gates are opened in Edinburgh. A great wistaria grew in the garden, and round this tree Alison and Francis executed an impromptu ballet dance to perplex the Scandinavians. Here they took their books and Francis watched Alison studying and sometimes started a discussion ("I admire Lytton Strachey, she doesn't.") and other times decided he had no business to talk to her.

About the middle of June one of the little Cremers became indisposed, and Madame was more than usually pressed for time. She made a proposal to the six pensionnaires, that they should take some picnic food, enough for a couple of days, and go to see Belle-Ile. It would be a pity to leave Nantes without seeing the pearl of Brittany. So early on a Saturday morning they set off – 19 June 1921. If there is any one date on which Alison's life changed course, this was it. They caught the daily boat at Quiberon for Le Palais, in very fine weather which continued arrogantly throughout the whole midsummer week-end. In Alison's description of it all when we met in August 1921, in Francis' nearly half a century later, the dominant impression was of timelessness. The days were unbroken by classes or duties or meal-times. Hour after hour they walked by the shore and the cliffs. They bathed, they lay in the sun talking and laughing together; and the deep immemorial chorus of the Atlantic rollers never ceased. More rugged than Berwickshire, more pagan and primitive, Belle-Ile seemed to Alison as magical as the Sutherland coast, that Back of the North Wind, the home of the Highland aunts.

They spent the first night in the inn at Sauzon and watched the moon rise. Francis painted the scene from memory afterwards

23

and it was this painting that Alison cherished most among all the keepsakes of the holiday. Sarah Bernhardt was living in retirement in her château nearby and next day Francis boldly walked up to the open door and looked in, while Alison and Graham peered from behind the laurel bushes in the drive. The party from the presbytery had already split, for Alison and Francis could not have too much solitude and wildness and wished to walk by the cliffs to Kervilahène, where the inn was reputed to be clean although somewhat rough and simple. Graham would stay in tow. But the Swedes found Belle-Ile just like Norway, "pas intéressante," besides, uncivilized. They retired for the day to Le Palais, and when they came back in the evening, refused to sleep at Kervilahène, and invited Alison to return to Le Palais with them by wagon. But Alison had been too happy all day, and she took a bold stand. She would stay on, unchaperoned, not the two nights that Francis and Graham planned to spend there, but just this one Sunday night. In the morning the wagon could fetch her to join the Swedes at Le Palais and catch the boat for Quiberon. This was the first unguarded move which made all the others possible.

The two rooms which they had taken were one above the other in a little cottage standing apart from the inn itself. In an artless snapshot it looks very like a disused stable, but Francis has assured me it was built as a cottage, although sometimes used as a haybarn. The lower room had no window, only a double door, but a vine and a red rose were growing up the front wall. From the upper room – which contained a bicycle standing upside down on its snowy boards – you looked out on the Atlantic itself. The young men decided that Alison should have the cottage to herself and sleep upstairs, and after locking her in they walked down the meadow towards the sea to find a bed among the ferns, and there they lay talking together until the first lark rose. At seven they called Alison to come and bathe, waking her by throwing roses through her bedroom window.

The wagon was due to come after lunch, which they ate at the inn (with a bottle of white wine), still in the highest spirits. But after lunch Francis went off without a word; Alison supposed he might be overcome with sleep. Eventually the wagon appeared, and Francis reappeared, but both so late that there was time merely for hurried farewells. Mme l'Hermite of the inn and all the friendly Bretons gathered round while Alison quickly clambered into her place, waving and calling "Ah, mais je reviendrai un jour!" It was a promise which the two boys relished, for they had contrived that her return should be much sooner than she expected. After lunch Francis had run two kilometres to waylay the driver of the wagon, who was easily persuaded to loiter until Alison was sure to miss the boat at Le Palais. The boys retired to sleep in the upper room at the cottage, suspecting that for the ordeal of confession they might need refurbishing. But a near-disaster at the inn played into their hands. At the very moment of Alison's return after missing the boat, one of the village children fell in the road, severing the artery in her wrist on a piece of broken glass. Francis and Graham heard Alison calling them urgently to come and help. In this sudden emergency the Bretons were dismayed and it was Alison who took charge and made a tourniquet with a rag and Francis' Venus pencil, and stopped the flow of blood. The fainting child (who had the charming name of Fortunée le Matelot) was carried on a mattress to the inn, and after a little the doctor came and pronounced her out of danger. Then Alison was thanked again and praised by all, and as soon as they could the three foreigners slipped away to take up the threads of their comedy in a hayfield. Alison was astounded to hear that she had been tricked into returning – amused, shocked, chagrined – then amused again that the daughter of a Scottish professor of Theology ("eminently respectable") should find herself in such a compromising situation. "There came a great many Oh's," ringing all the changes of her inner reactions with wonderful precision and attack. At dinner they could talk of nothing else but the great Blague. Alison refused to say that she was glad to be there, and tried to speak seriously, but there was much laughter.

When Tuesday came they set out to walk the six kilometres to Palais under the full blaze of the summer solstice. Francis noted gratefully that Alison never flagged and never said she was thirsty. The sea was choppy and her pallor disturbed him, but remembering what his parents had done once when he came back from South Kensington Museum in an exhausted state, he asked at the station inn at Quiberon for some brandy, tasted a drop and knew by "the hot effect" that it was right, and took the potion to Alison. Her colour returned and they arrived back cheerfully at the presbytery to find Madame in no way put out by what had happened. It was the first time Alison had tasted brandy and weeks later when she told me the story of Belle-Ile, the miraculous power of liquor was given special mention. And Sarah Bernhardt! Almost as soon as they were back, she emerged from her château and appeared in the theatre at Nantes sitting under a trellis covered with roses, herself so rouged and bewigged that she blossomed too. Her voice, at first low and uncertain, as she gave her recitations, gained in strength until it filled the theatre.

> Je t'adore Soleil! Tu mets dans l'air des roses,
> Des flammes dans la source, un dieu dans le buisson!
> Tu prends un arbre obscur et tu l'apothéoses!

There were ten more days for Alison and Francis. Graham left first, for Switzerland, and was the first to suffer from the separation. Two years later he wrote to Alison "It is absolutely impossible for me to describe my wretchedness on the Swiss tour." Alison was to leave Nantes on July 5 for a week in Paris, and Francis was accompanying the Cremers to the Bas-Pyrénées. On July 4 he and Alison took a last walk through the countryside of their first outings. This time they went to visit one of the Cremer daughters at a farm some miles from the town, but they lost their way and were benighted. Francis afterwards tried to map their looped wanderings, miles of rough dark walking through which he was sustained by the delight of Alison's company. But Alison was exhausted long before they reached Nantes again, and in a panic when at last in the small hours of the morning Francis rang the bell in the iron door in the garden wall of 24 rue de Gigant. The Cremers were waiting up, Madame in her nightdress, both of them vexed and worried. There was no opportunity for second thoughts or discussion under less agitating circumstances, for in a few hours Alison had packed up and left for Paris. Something convinced her that this last adventure would not escape censure. The great Blague on Belle-Ile might by itself have passed, while losing their way and returning so late could happen to anyone, but to a critical or apprehensive adult the two events were certain to knock the innocence out of each other. In a few days however she had recovered her poise and was writing to me on the back of the Victory "I can't believe I'm me." It was the novelty of it all that overwhelmed her, being on her own with two young men, among the Breton fisher people on their Atlantic island. She hardly collected her wits to measure Francis, that brilliant and uncompromising personality, or even to ask herself what was the nature of their attachment.

Francis wrote to his parents on July 12 from Osse-près-Bedouse in the Bas-Pyrenées. He and the Cremer family had travelled in a third class railway carriage packed like sardines, "and oh that 3 hours 'travers des Landes' where even the wind is filled with hot sand. We were nearly dead when we got here." Osse was not a good place to continue his studies – a valley shut in by mountains where "from 11/clock to 7/clock no-one moves for fear of sweating and sunstroke," and at night there were only candles to read by. He fell ill and Madame put him on a diet and kept him in bed until he recovered. Some friendly Irish people were also staying in the village but "not at all literary, and I longed for Alison. They kept on thinking about omelettes at Urdos. Though kindness itself, I could not help a sort of internal vomit at the thought of omelettes when there were great eagles soaring overhead. Alison and I would have gone mad with joy and adventure." He felt that his parents knew her already. Would they please send all cuttings on the strength or weakness of Wirth's Cabinet, the Anglo-Jap Treaty and the possible removal of Kemal to Constantinople. It was a very long letter and his third to them in three days. The day that he wrote it, Alison left Paris to join her father in London and go with him to Farnham Castle where they were guests of Bishop Talbot, "the most angelic old bishop." She still believed that Belle-Ile had been the rock from which she leaped into life – as Corsica was

to Boswell – and walking on the lawns among the roses at
Farnham Castle she poured out the whole story of the past
seven weeks to her father, hoping that he would agree that such
Wordsworthian bliss was permissible on earth, that there were
times and situations so pure and rare as to sanction the throbbing
of the heart. But he listened with mounting dismay. To him
Alison seemed to have been in considerable peril. He knew that
she was naturally a rebel and a sceptic, and this young man had
broken the rules. Helen Cairns I think might have looked at it
rather differently. So much nearer to her daughter in age (had
she lived) she would have listened in sympathy and passed on
what was suitable to the over-anxious father – as our own
mother did when we confided in her. Even with us however
Alison's adventures would at that date have seemed unconven-
tional, and D. S. Cairns was still very near to the traditions of
his peasant ancestors and to the iron discipline which must have
prevailed in the cottage at Dunglass. In those narrow quarters
nothing else was compatible with decency and godliness, and
the young John Cairns in sole charge of the school at Ayton when
he was seventeen, belaboured his pupils so that they remembered
it all their lives. Daughters from such a home were never without
protection. If they left their parents it was to marry or to live
with relatives or persons who could be as wholly trusted as
relatives. It is impossible for us to see the serious and idealistic
Francis as dangerous, but Alison was impressed by something
patrician in his ways of living and thinking, and passed on to
her father (and others) the notion that Francis belonged to a
different world with different standards. Rather adroitly however, D. S. Cairns avoided discussion of conventions and the
awful facts behind conventions. He brought her to consider
how selfish she and Francis had been in forgetting that the
Cremers were poor, and depended upon their pensionnaires to
make ends meet. *Their* reputation might be damaged if the
story got around. Alison was soon restored to the old and credible
view of herself as the professor's daughter, eminently respectable.
It was a victory for parental anxiety, an easy victory already
half-won in absentia, for why else had the bell in the garden gate
of the presbytery sounded so terrible at three in the morning that

Alison shook with apprehension, "a hideous little coward" as she called herself in later years? Francis would willingly have set every bell in Nantes ringing, woken every sleeper without compunction. It was Francis whom she had let down, and her own panic that she hated to remember, but the parental view of the affair helped to gloss over her humiliation. So she sat down to write the first letter. The detailed account of her week in Paris for which Francis was waiting was never written at all. She made a reference to the heat and dust, and the lightest reference to Belle-Ile – how remembering the freshness of it made Paris seem all the hotter and dustier. Then "I want to be absolutely frank with you" – words to put even the most devoted friend on guard. "About that last night at Nantes. You know that half of my mind seemed simply to be somewhere else, where or why I can't imagine, but it does sometimes, generally when I'm tired. I know that you were on the very heights, but somehow I wasn't. I don't think you saw that, and that's what made me feel such a hypocrite as we were coming down into Nantes. Another thing that I can't forget is that we let the Cremers down so badly. . . ."

This was the letter that Francis opened with passionate eagerness in the steaming pocket of Osse. "I grew up considerably in the reading of that letter." He took it as a repudiation of something unique and beautiful in both their lives, for it had been a time of fresh-sprung sympathy such as one marvels to imagine. I wrote in an earlier version of this story that it was not the Cremers, or Francis even, who suffered most but Alison herself, and this brought from Francis a hot marginal denial, for he became ill with misery and left the Cremers after ten days. But indeed it *was* in the long run Alison who suffered most. At Francis' request Mme Cremer wrote to Alison to reassure her. Madame certainly had made it easy for him to ask such a favour, for she had turned to the stricken young man on the railway platform at Nantes, as the train bearing Alison steamed out, pronouncing these conclusive words: "Oui, elle n'est pas une jeune fille quelconque!" She also wrote a delightful letter to Francis a couple of weeks after he had returned to England. "Nous serons toujours heureux d'avoir de vos nouvelles et nous gardons de vous le meilleur souvenir. J'ai écrit comme je vous l'avais promis, disant à Alison qu'elle ne devait plus penser à cette histoire."

But in the Cairns family it was less easily forgotten. D. S. Cairns set himself to protect Alison from herself and from others for as long as might be necessary. She did not talk about this and at first perhaps hardly realized how much her freedom was curtailed. The following Christmas vacation she and I made plans to spend two weeks at Easter in Somerset, lodging in a farmhouse. Everything was in train and the prospect enchanting, when my father brought me a message from D. S. Cairns that it was all off. He thought it risky for two young women (20 and 19 at that time) to go away without an older woman in charge. My parents were surprised and my mother wondered if he had heard stories about undesirable men lurking behind Somerset hedges. Francis, as little aware of these undercurrents as I or my parents, visited Alison at Girton and introduced her to his favourite uncle, and in 1922 when Alison was abroad he stayed with Graham on Deeside and called on D. S. Cairns, to be received with "grave courtesy and charm" which revealed no criticism. Nevertheless meetings were not encouraged by the Cairns family. When Francis visited relatives in the Lake District, although Alison was staying nearby with her aunt and uncle at Lochton, no invitation came from the Aitchisons to the young man. Harder still, when he won a university prize, there was no money available for Alison to travel to Oxford to attend the prize-giving, although it had been while walking along the Backs with her at Cambridge that he had thrashed out his ideas for the successful entry. There was however no embargo upon letters.

WHEN I turn over the pages of the Girton College Register, I think that Alison was fortunate to go up when she did. Many names catch the eye. There was Iso Brown, for instance, who hated it all even more than Alison and left after a year, and between 1939 and 1946 housed and cared for forty-three unwanted babies, adopting four of them; Alison's cousin, the beautiful Rosemary Blackadder from Chirnside who became the Princess von Urach; another rare beauty, Rosamund Lehmann, on the brink of writing one of the most successful novels of the early twenties; Sylvia Fletcher-Moulton; Joan Maurice (afterwards Robinson) the economist; Margaret Horsey, the psychologist and humanist, who married Rex Knight; Alice Walter, afterwards Mrs MacNabb MacLeod of MacLeod, who was to win the Kaisar-I-Hind Gold Medal and live in Dunvegan Castle. But neither from Alison's conversation nor from her letters did I gather that she found the company very congenial or stimulating. She complained "at college it's impossible to think." Hardly any of the lectures seemed worth attending. "I cut right and left and feel I could cut all with profit." Cambridge itself was a consolation but not the Cambridgeshire countryside. "The trees are stockish even in the strongest gale and the water lies stagnant in the ditches." Her sense of anti-climax was shared by Graham at Oxford. All her life she kept a short letter from him, written in his first term, with a simplicity and force so much less common than the anguish which he describes.

"I find I must write to someone for want of having anyone to speak to. I think in all I have uttered three words to-day and each time the same thing: 'thank you.' Really life here is awful. There does not seem to be anybody who has not plenty of friends without me. So in my usual, perhaps foolish way I leave everyone

31

unmolested and suffer accordingly. It is not in my nature to push myself in when other people are getting on gloriously without me. From this loneliness comes the natural result, I sit down to read Rousseau's Contrat Social and find myself sleeping under the midnight sky of Kervilahen. Oh it is miserable. And my examination is in three weeks."

Francis, of the three the one most deeply involved in the Belle-Ile adventure, was yet the happiest and most successful in his university years. Both his seniors and his contemporaries were impressed by him. He had a public life in which he blossomed, and for his deeper, private emotions he found solace in writing, particularly in the task of putting his memories of the spring and summer at Nantes into a form half fiction and half fact. He was Coningsby, Alison, Junia, and the completed work, *Le Conte de Six Semaines*, arrived in Alison's pigeon hole by the office of the admirable Emily, the portress, in January of 1924. It was a wonderful gift, and for a time lifted her out of the depression and boredom of her college years.

"On the first Sunday of term I threw open my windows, pulled my deepest armchair round into the sun, and turned to the April which did not belong but could not be left out of it. [Francis had preceded Alison at Nantes, and arrived in April.] In one hour I only read a very few pages – this was for several reasons. First of all the fields, where you began, then the Rue de Gigant, then the exhilaration and feeling of endless possibilities that you communicate, O most *admirably*. Lastly the most amazing experience in my own mind – quite suddenly all the muddled ideas and all the confusion of experience, which had been accumulating for years, arranged themselves and leapt together. . . . 'So *this* is life, so *this* is God' I exclaimed irreverently! I turned again and again to the pages on the Loire valley and to April. I enjoyed myself so much that the critical devil of which I'm possessed went to sleep."*

If there was any recantation still needed for the prim little note she had posted to Osse, here it was. Francis must have been pleased, and perhaps he was satisfied. He kept the letter as

---

* Alison to Francis from Girton, 22 February 1924. Her irreverences of 1924 were to become respectable theology in less than thirty years.

he kept every line that she wrote to him, but the new era that it heralded was still postponed. At the end of this term Alison and I went away together – without any chaperon, although not to a remote farmhouse in exotic Somerset, but to rooms let by Miss Isabella Beattie in Braemar. On the first of April it was still winter there, with no flowers and little grass. The hungry deer slipped across the deserted roads a few yards ahead of us, with a delicacy that masked their haste.

"I had never been among the hills at that time of year before and was enchanted. All the higher hills were white and the lower ones ribbed and streaked with snow. Great patches of snow lay on the moors and along by the burns. You can't conceive of the queer *intimate* feeling it gives to stick your hand into a snow-wreath, while an April sun beats on your head and a cold wind blows off the hills through plantings of old grey twisted birches. The strange people and creatures of the Celtic twilight type became possible – they always annoyed me rather till then. One day we spied a webbed foot-mark in the snow beside a burn! The friend I was with was of the most entirely congenial. We talked about people and literature ad infin. with many lucid intervals of ribaldry. We rubbed off each other's corners beautifully; she kept me in my place and I stopped her exclaiming at the Beauties of Nature. This is a mutual agreement between David and me, that we shall not except in the rarest circumstances, call each other's attentions to sunsets etc."*

We took the *Daily Mirror* each day, since Alison could not live without the comic strip *Pip, Squeak and Wilfrid*, and so we came to read the current Mirror serial, which provoked most of the ribaldry she mentions. Its author was a girl of seventeen, Mollie Panter-Downes, who then proceeded to grow and slough new skins with such rapidity that she soon graduated to the *New Yorker* and by her suave London Letters probably did more to bring America into the war on our side than any other journalist. I remember the ban on talk of Beauty, but not how I kept Alison in her place, wherever that was, nor the rubbing off of corners. But she did put *me* in *my* place some years later, in a way that I never forgot. We were riding on the top of a London bus to-

* Alison to Francis from Girton, 10 May 1924

gether and she pointed out that a remark I had made in a newspaper article was smug. This was obvious as soon as she mentioned it, and for smugness there is never any excuse. Next morning there was a letter from Alison in the post, apologizing for her smugness in rebuking me for mine. She often wondered if she were too outspoken, but her criticisms were always without animosity, indeed they were prompted by affection and concern.

After the last term at Girton, Alison's plans for visits to Oxford and elsewhere were spoilt by an outbreak of German measles and she returned to Aberdeen, to 139 Desswood Place – the "rather horrid little house," which her father had recently bought – and described herself as "really withered with disappointment," without any idea when she would find an excuse to go south again. Her lot now seemed to be cast in Aberdeen for an indefinite time. The skimpy front garden of 139 was wedged with melancholy shrubs, which made David's room and the drawing-room damp, but as they obscured the view of the houses across the road, Alison let them be. Two rooms on the first floor were thrown together to make a sizable study for D. S. Cairns, for whom no study ever provided enough level surface. Alison's own room was on the second floor looking south over houses and gardens. A photograph of her mother stood on a bow-fronted chest of drawers, and the sense of privacy, up there in the quiet top storey of a house that was never noisy, compensated to some extent for the chilly and impersonal atmosphere of the rooms below.

Alison had been awarded second class honours in both parts of the tripos (Medieval and Modern Languages), but she never for a moment doubted that Francis would get a first and return to Oxford for a fourth year. It was not until September that a letter reached her with the news that he too had been placed in the second class, and was leaving England for Rhodesia. She described herself as "quite strange and staggered with it all." She wanted to come south and see him before he sailed, but again she had to say it was impossible. She tried to encourage him. The Jews, she believed, must have meant adventure when they spoke of faith. "I seem to remember a long chapter which used to bore us very much when read at prayers, the 'By faith' one from one of the epistles, Hebrews I think. Only adventure is better than faith." At this moment when the indefinable bond between them was to be tested in a new and rigorous fashion, Alison allowed herself unusual warmth and freedom. "I have never met anyone else yet who had an enchanted six weeks have you?"

This was the sum of her three years' experience. And after the discovery that, like Christmas at Lochton in her childhood, Belle-Ile had no parallel in the lives of her friends, there followed the unwelcome suspicion that it might be unparalleled in her own life too. "Ah, mais je reviendrai un jour," but she never did, neither to the island itself, nor by any other gateway to a time of such exalted spirits. Yet it was not a dream, but "ten times realer than the dustiness and fustiness of things," substantiated by precious tokens from time to time, a letter for example from Fortunée le Matelot – a most delicately penned and worded letter (headed *Grand-Phare*) thanking all three for a Christmas parcel. Graham alone had recovered his composure. He wrote to Alison: "It hardly seems like four years and more since I was in France but during that time much has happened. We three have passed through an English University. Francis has not done so well yet as I then thought he would. I have learned many lessons since then but none the less I shall for ever look back to June 1921 as one of the most romantic periods of my life."

After the first shock of knowing that Francis was emigrating (his destination was changed from Rhodesia to New Zealand) Alison began to feel some envy. "I suppose you won't come home for years, by which time you will be too famous to be approachable, and I shall be a heavy British matron. xxxxxxxxxx Under these scratches I had written 'with crowds of horrid little children' but decided that would really be too dismal to speak about."

To me she did deplore having been born a woman, but I had been reading Benjamin Kidd's *The Science of Power* and quoted "Woman is the psychic centre of social integration," for what comfort it could give her. She thanked me with unusual earnestness. Society has not yet integrated very much, in spite of its psychic centre, but I found and Alison did too, that while the Brotherhood of Man is no more than a distant hope, the Sisterhood of Women is a present reality.

35

Before Francis sailed, Alison sent him a manuscript book, copying out on the first of its pages all four stanzas of the song from "Prometheus Unbound," Act II, Scene V.

> Life of Life! thy lips enkindle
>   With their love the breath between them. . . .
> Lamp of Earth! where'er thou movest
>   Its dim shapes are clad with brightness,
> And the souls of whom thou lovest
>   Walk upon the winds with lightness
> Till they fail as I am failing,
> Dizzy, lost, yet unbewailing!

He was deeply impressed and grateful. His own parting gift to her, finished the night before he left and posted after he had gone, was a second even more finely-wrought version of *Le Conte de Six Semaines* between linen covers and illustrated with his own water-colours. Alison now wrote rather more frequently, and her letters supported him while he came to terms with life in a young and hard-headed country. At the end of one there is a faint pencil note written by Francis on its reception in New Zealand in 1925. "April 22 Eve of Patron Saint. Two letters come again. Extraordinary change of heart after reading them. Courage returns."

AFTER Cambridge, Alison took stock of her education. She had acquired a better than average knowledge of French, both language and literature, and of English literature and history. And either at the Mount or at Girton she had learned to talk with an English accent and lost the distinctive warmth of tone of the educated Scot: this did not worry her, perhaps she had done it deliberately. Her chief criticism was the neglect of the senses. "Art – save the word – is not taught as having any connection with life and things and pleasure. Lord I boil to think of the dismal hours I spent drawing beer bottles, and boxes cornerwise on; and the less dismal but more heated half hours when I launched vicious kicks at my music mistress's piano – and hang it all, of course I was right." But in fairness to at least one of her Art mistresses, I should say that I am still reaping the benefit of her simple instructions about looking at nature, choosing and mixing colours, and recording in pencil and paint what is seen. We all started with the same Music mistress, Daisy Matthews, who took me to the first opera I ever experienced, and it was an experience – *Madame Butterfly*. My younger sister Yda was well on the way to giving herself and others musical pleasure before she graduated from Daisy to more sophisticated teachers. The diluted sweetness of those vacant years still hangs about the memory of Yda's playing César Franck in the music room at the manse; while the evening sunshine crept round to pierce the screen of trees and flutter above her shining head. Alison was not as unmusical as Great-uncle John, whose repertoire began and ended with the Old Hundredth, but she was by nature far less sensitive to music than to words. (With the majority the reverse is true.) Without David's interest, his piano playing, and his gramophone records of Wagner's operas, she might never have felt her education inadequate for the ear. On the domestic side of life, she stood self-condemned – "I am one of nature's sluts" – and looking over my shoulder in the kitchen said pensively "So that's how you poach an egg." But her greatest handicap was ignorance of the limits of her own strength. In the old days people always walked from Berwickshire to Edinburgh, and the idea lingered on that everyone ought to be able to walk fifty miles in a day. D. S. Cairns had cured himself of dyspepsia and insomnia by walking.

But as her father's daughter she became the Moderator's lady in 1923–4 and learned all the skills of a good hostess. She was never visibly embarrassed, always interested, her courtesy from the heart. Unfortunately the salon was an institution unknown in Aberdeen and almost dead in Edinburgh, for she was admirably suited to lead the most brilliant and delightful of salons. If friendship is a vocation, she did not regard it so, rather as a form of self-indulgence – or at least her need rather than that of others. Notions about filling time suitably – and what is suitable in so vast and mysterious a context? – of amassing knowledge, having a career, were at that time axioms of existence. The Bible, Spenser and Bunyan had created for us a parabolic conception of the self as a triumvirate, mind, soul and heart, living uneasily together inside the body (something not quite right, but exonerated by clothing) and supplied with the talents as working capital. When Alison began to brood upon what she called a sense of reality these myths proved formidable obstacles to a happy issue. She could look back to experiences of reality, at Foulden as a little girl, and on Belle-Ile, but at Girton the pump had been "aff the fang." Even if she had seen herself as indivisible, a functioning person, the conditions in which to function were lacking. She admired my mother's vitality beyond bounds ("I *dote* on your mother – I have never met anyone like her – have you?") and cultivated her to discover the secret; but my mother, all innocence and appetite, had never any conception of what Alison was going through. Terms like real and unreal would have puzzled her – philosophical distinctions – for with five surviving children, some already married, grandchildren coming, she was never left alone to know a hollow moment. If cross-examined, she probably would have said that life was altogether too real for her liking, and the bites that seemed play and pretence drew blood every time. David had now gone up to Balliol and I was doing post-graduate work at Girton, and in Aberdeen Alison lacked young company, but she fought her melancholy – as people were urged to do in those days – and developed a life-long severity towards her own moods and an exquisite sympathy for other people in the same plight. Yda, who also ate her heart out there in the early twenties, used to go to a film or a party with Alison and walk home with her, and then Alison turned to walk home with Yda, and then if it were not too late they would retrace the familiar walk, down the hill by Dalgarno's Nurseries and up Desswood Place to the end, amusing and encouraging one another as they went, although Yda was ignorant too of the depth of Alison's unhappiness. Her liveliness and ready spontaneous laughter were completely deceiving. How fatal it is to climb down decorously from a splendid romance, as she did in the rose garden at Farnham Castle. To crash is far better. If she had crashed at least she would have known what Conrad called "that special intensity of existence which is the quintessence of youthful aspirations."

Even in the Highlands on holiday Alison was troubled by a "kind of hardness, an insensitive crust" which did not prevent her from seeing beauty but robbed her of any delight in it. She railed against the conventionality of the people she met. "Why are they so unreal? Do they like to be?" she wrote to me in desperation, and to Francis "I long for really congenial work and friends. I yearn for dances and charming young men. Of these *non pas* – or in small measure." She thought this was peculiar to the north of Scotland, forgetting what had befallen all the seed of Europe, one by one, and was even haunted by the idea that a woman who did not marry had herself to blame; she had failed in some way. The one Aberdeen friendship that promised for a time to ripen, shrivelled on the bough, and the holiday on Belle-Ile shone like its own lighthouse exposing the tawdriness of many opportunities. School and college friends came north and amused her as much as she amused them with

39

gay and witty conversation, and then to her amazement David would complain that he found one or another of those chosen companions unreal and impossible to get to know, and D. S. Cairns infuriated them both by enquiring "Has he (or she) *developed?*"

But this aspect of D. S. Cairns was one that I rarely noticed. He delighted us always with his powers of entertainment, thinking up and acting a piece of wonderful mockery, pulling out poetry and ghost stories and memories of the great from his fabulous store, expounding an historical theory as if his immortal soul depended upon its truth. Yet he had a fearfulness about life. In the end he overcame it, but in his early years and even his middle age it was an obstinate fearfulness; and of course he had the elderly scholar's habits, absorption in his work and general short sight. *Middlemarch*, so Alison told me once, had been a book which helped her mother, for she recognised some similarities between Dorothea's married life and her own. A man capable of shaking hands with the ticket collector on the train, and carrying on his conversation without a notion of what the outheld hand meant, could not become perceptive the instant that he stepped over the threshold into his own house. After the little act with which he greeted me in the street, tapping my shoulder and saying "Be virtuous and you will be happy," we parted without being a whit wiser about one another. It was a gesture courteously evolved to tide over the impossible business of breaking through to an inarticulate child.

Very few young men were even on the *short leet* as marriageable in Alison's family or mine. Family tradition required a suitor to be middle class, tending to upper rather than lower. Parental anxiety insisted upon his being a church-goer, unsmirched by the world, and in steady employment. But we girls looked for vitality, polish, a pleasant appearance, and brains. Candidates to satisfy both sets of examiners were not very plentiful. Francis certainly, was always on the *short leet*, perhaps always at the head of the list, although the scepticism which endeared him to Alison counted against him with D. S. Cairns. But a crust had formed here too. The friendship (so much of it on paper) was becoming too well-established, and its terms of reference set.

ALISON CAIRNS

So Alison occupied herself running a dramatic group for the high-spirited members of a club for working girls, and took classes at the university, playing with the idea of a post-graduate degree. At 139 Desswood Place she set herself to get her father's correspondence under control. In the "seas and tides of papers that ebbed and flowed" on the study table she used to come upon old letters of her own and re-read them as a discipline. Some of her early letters to Francis now make heavy enough reading, and he warned her about flatness with acerbity that "served to season two or three insipid days." But a change came in 1926 when Alison went for a couple of weeks to France and spent a night with the Cremers – now at Châlons-sur-Marne. Although the town and the presbytery were different, much was the same – the weak tea and the quince jam, the Bible laid out on an embroidered mat and the histories of the *bonnes à tout faire*. ("Et sur ce mot exquis elle nous a quitté . . .") Yet one enormous change – the family Cremer which had formerly been outside the enchanted circle was now inside. "Madame is more wonderful than ever." Graham had sent them *Punch* every week since he left, every week for five years. "C'est au fond un garçon vraiment gentil," said Madame, but the drollness of it had not passed her by. "It was an extraordinarily happy visit," Alison wrote to Francis, "how lucky and happy one feels when one's anticipations are fulfilled and more than fulfilled." No outraged British parents had boycotted the pastor and his wife. The summer of five years ago took on a new authenticity – remembrance was transformed from dwelling on the past to something astonishingly near to living it again. Listen to her letter on Midsummer Day that year.

"C'est aujourd'hui le jour de la Grande Blague. I have just come back to Kevilahène and injured and angry, am haranguing you and Graham in the little space between our cottage and the screen of big willow shoots between it and the hayfield. I'm trying to remember if I came back suspicious or unsuspecting, the latter I think, but I can't remember the moment of revelation. I remember you were wily enough to say 'Now I wonder if she's going to see the funny side or not,' and of course I laughed, a little because I did, but mostly because I didn't like it thought that there was a funny side I wasn't seeing. Funny, I remember that was the second time I fell into that same little snare of yours. The first was under the trees in the garden at 24 when Elizabeth and I were a little peevish because we thought Madame was pushing us off to Belle Isle. Most people would rather have it hinted that they were deficient in a sense of honour than in a sense of humour.

"You know, that sketch of yours in the Conte of the moon coming up over the Sauzon cliffs gives me, more than anything, the feeling of the time. That was one of the moments when the sense of Romance was strongest, – the strangeness of *me* being *there*. And again the next night when you and Graham had locked me up in the Kervilahène cottage for the night, and I stood half out of the window and heard your steps and noises die away, and looked out upon the night and the moonlight and the willows and the sea, I think that was the most amazing and lovely moment of all. Yes I think it was, it was the most adventurous, tho' as I write picture after picture and moment after moment come to mind and ask to be recorded as such. – And then waking up next morning and opening one's eyes to red roses lying on the floor.

"By the way do you remember much of the conversation of those days? I remember saying irritably to you on the Sunday afternoon when we spread ourselves out on the Danish camp or barrow 'O you're *much* too subtle!' but à propos of what? And after I had bathed on the Monday morning, drying my hair in the sun, while the three of us sat on the rocks, weak and helpless with laughter at each others' observations on the inmates of 24.

"*Later.* By now we have staunched Fortunée's wound, and reconciled, have fed, and are looking for glow-worms. Do you remember the scents of hay this night? and the cool, lonely air?"*

This was the year that she believed she was recovering "morally and intellectually" from her three years at Girton – "where I was deeply and dreadfully bored – most of the time. And there is nothing so demoralising and disintegrating as boredom – nothing so unhappy. It's better to be hurt than to be bored." Girton had to take the blame for the over-all structure of those years, and yet it was in her room at Girton she sat

* Alison to Francis from Aberdeen, 21 June 1926

reading the *Conte de Six Semaines* and exclaimed "So this is God."
A few months later she wrote to Francis:

"I have felt lately that something might 'click' quite soon,
and the dislocated parts might fall into place. I wish I could
think the process was intellectual, for I should be more sure of
its consummation, but alas 'tis obscure and its workings very
doubtful. . . . No, I don't want life to be a fairy-tale, I want it
to be a constant sense of reality – which is only rare and inter-
mittent with me now." She envied Francis deeply for his faculty
of delight, the beginning of wisdom. Then he was incapable of
being all things to all men. But "I can be a great many things to
a great many different men – it's a kind of easy surface enjoyment
and sympathy, not without its own value." She saw him as
always ready to sacrifice himself for his ideals. "I've never had
to act on such perceptions, if I had I honestly don't think I
should care a damn for what people thought." And she added,
as if their memories had become a crucible, "Don't judge me
please by Belle-Ile and Mme Charpiot, I was timidly taking
refuge in an attitude then, I think, that wasn't really my own
(so that of course made me the hideous little coward I was when
the Gigant bell clanged at 3 a.m.)"

She watched the afternoon light of the October day ebbing
away over the roof-tops from her bedroom window. "It was like
watching something turning almost miraculously into a quite
other thing . . ." and her handwriting suddenly spread and
sprawled all over the page with excitement. "I don't think I
shall be happy till I feel I know *every*thing and understand
*every*thing and experience *every*thing."*

---

* Alison to Francis from Aberdeen, 9 October 1926. Alison's punctuation and
spelling is throughout this book exactly as I found it in her letters and any mistakes
she made are left intact and without comment, but I have replaced the truncated
form of '&' which she used by 'and'.

THE MORE hopelessly Alison pursued reality, the harder she found it to be in sympathy with Christianity. (Dostoevski says that a man must love life before he can love the meaning of life.) Finally she confessed herself a pagan. Among all her relatives and all the known ancestors for many generations, only her great-grandfather James Craw had doubted the truth of Christianity and (although in time his faith returned) had continued to hold aloof from the church. Alison chose the term pagan deliberately, to convey that she was not an atheist nor even an agnostic, but merely an outsider. "I love the sound of church bells – when I can swing on a gate and watch other people going to church." But she was awkwardly placed for gate-swinging in a country where royal ancestry can be passed over more easily than direct descent from John Brown of Haddington. No Scot is surprised by the remark of the Aberdeen taxi-driver to the American scholar in search of D. S. Cairns – "Aye, ye'll be meaning the professor of Apologetics and Dogmatics." Fortunately by this time her father too had travelled a long way since he wrote the children his earnest exhortation in 1916, and he showed no concern when Alison said that perhaps after his death she might become a Christian, but at present she felt that it was all being done for her. David was different – he had always been different – and when he entered the ministry, it took some of the sting out of Alison's defection, or so she thought and hoped.

She was relieved to come out in the open and dissociate herself from a good deal of solemnity and from the kind of person she once cruelly described as "shabby, sheepish, pious and ineffective – everything I most dislike." Relieved, but not jubilant, for oddly enough very few with any experience of believing, even at second hand, find scepticism a happy state,

44

while the completion of the reverse journey, from doubting to believing is as a rule bliss. The confession of unfaith had been brought to a head by an invitation to D. S. Cairns from the World Student Federation to spend six months of 1927 visiting universities and mission stations in China and Japan. Alison was invited too, as his secretary, and she was determined to forestall misunderstanding, knowing that wherever they went it would be taken for granted that her father's daughter was rooted and grounded in her father's faith. "There are so few Christians," she wrote to Francis, "who don't become a little restrained when they find out that you're not one of them, slightly reproving, or slightly shocked, or slightly uncomfortable – oh damn them what right have they." But when she reached the mission fields first in Japan, and then China, she liked the missionaries. They were good company, "alive and pleasant and real," and took no umbrage at all, unlike the good people at home. They had chosen to live in pagan countries; she was no novelty to them – as far as her disbelief went.

"The most genuinely thrilling moment of our travels was, I think, landing in Korea at Fusan. Till then we had been among our own kind and a good part of the time actually with friends. At last we were completely cut off. We arrived about 7 o'clock in the glare of a peculiarly cold bright colourless sunset, the sun having just gone down behind the most distant of range upon range of sharp cardboard-like mountains. These broke down to the sea in great bluffs and precipices with twisted firs along their spines and a heavy green sea breaking whitely along their bases. O I tell you it was queer arriving at the end of the world like that and one thought went beating round inside my mind, like a bat – Asia – Asia – Asia. When you got close to the wharf the oddest looking people were crowding down, tall, yellow, slant-eyed in white Biblical robes, and the most absurd little hats like baby silk hats (the funeral kind), but perched upon the very top of the head and tied with strings beneath the chin."*

From Korea they went inland to Manchuria and as far north as Kirin, "an old official town on the Sungari river (about 500 miles above the point where it joins the Amur) and capital

* Alison to Lyn from Shanghai, 3 June 1927

45

of the province of the same name. The Sungari is magnificent, and the town stretches for 5 miles on a bend of it, one-storey houses, with ribbony willows breaking their lines, then the river dull oxydised silver with colours changing continually beneath its surface, then wooded hills and mountains with quickly changing lights. Great timber-rafts with families and communities living on them came down the river, and rafts loaded with hay, a lovely rich colour when the sun struck it, only a little paler than the roofs of the Confucian temple that turned up its corners against the dark blue of wooded hills. And the streets – gay bright little thoroughfares with silk shops and fruit stalls, no motor cars only rickshaws and droskies with high yokes and two or three horses. You could get glimpses into private courtyards decked with oleanders, red and white, in pots, and geraniums and white nicotine flowers. The Chinese are for the most part a very fascinating-looking people, the men tall and slender with fine subtle features, and exquisite hands. They wear long straight white flowered-silk robes in summer (like cassocks) and panama hats with wavy brims, and as they walk they continually open and click shut their fans. Every now and then you see a lady with shallow bright-coloured silks, green ear-rings and white jade ornaments in her stiff shiny hair. I don't think there was a foreigner in the place excepting two or three missionaries, and three or four Russians, grooms to wealthy Chinese. Manchuria is full of White Russians. The fortunate ones keep little groceries or millinery shops where there is a foreign community as in Mukden, and at night have dinners and soirées in their old style, like the 18th century French emigrés in London. Harbin is full of them, and of Red Russians, plotting and counterplotting and killing each other in the streets all the time. We never got to Harbin, but strange wild stories were constantly being passed on about queer happenings in the North. One could buy Paris models up there for next to nothing, we heard, for they come out with opium stitched in hems and seams."*

Because of the threat of war D. S. Cairns wished to leave

---

* Alison to Francis from the S.S. Rawalpindi in the Straits of Malacca 27 August 1927

Alison behind, first in Tokyo and then in Mukden, but she was determined to go on with him, and when the southern armies started quarrelling among themselves, it was considered to be safe enough in Peking for a month or two. She loved Peking. She bought a pair of jade earrings, little fish dangling from a string of pearls, and danced until her gold slippers were almost worn out. The Peking missionaries took her to Wofussu and they slept out under the pines in a temple court "where stars like fruit were gleaming." In her diary which had begun fresh and vivid during a rough trans-Atlantic voyage, the writing grew smaller and more crabbed as the weeks and months passed and she laboured to keep level with the new experiences; every encounter, sight, event, every dance partner and every new sensation.

"These months have been a liberation for me, partly because the vast swarming numbers of Chinese (there are four hundred million of them) cheapen one's own sense of individual importance, and partly because they don't crowd in on one's consciousness as people do at home – they are so incomprehensible in their characters, the colours of their background, their classes and their occupations; they are men and not persons. And instead of wanting to read novels one wants to read histories; people in the mass and the movements and government of the mass have suddenly become interesting."*

While she was in Manchuria her enquiries had brought an offer of a foothold in Tokyo, and she made "the first really shattering decision" of her life – not to return to the west. "I saw quite definitely that I had to go and decided for it after much weighing. It was a plunge." But twelve hours later the decision was scrapped. "Francis, I am *not* a good daughter. I resented very much that phrase which you used in your last letter to me! Father and I are frequently at loggerheads – I have a fiendish and meanly irritable temper and I don't spare him much of it. But I am attached to the old dear and I can't let him go back after all the strain of the summer to a heavy winter and an uncertain menage. The news was that our excellent housekeeper couldn't come back. In a way I feel

* Alison to Francis from the Straits of Malacca, 27 August 1927

47

defeated, my plans *were* defeated, but I don't think I am. In those twelve hours I knew I could make up my mind to a thing, and decide to do it in spite of being horribly harrowed in my feelings. I shall go home now, but with the prospect of cutting away after the winter I think. Do think of something amusing for me to do after that!"

In June, she and her father had drawn penny-in-the-slot fortunes from a machine in the temple at Shinonoschi in Japan. "Mine said: 'You will be restless till you find God.' D.S.C.'s said: 'You have lost something important, but ask a woman to help you and you will find it' – a true word that!"

SO THE winter after the World Tour was spent at 139 Desswood Place. D. S. Cairns was at last writing the book on miracles which he had contemplated for nearly twenty years, and Alison hunted for the missing sheets of manuscript among the seas and tides of papers on the study table, and held him to his resolve. The work went ahead and the book was published in the spring of 1928 by the Student Movement Press under the title *The Faith that Rebels*. It was so well received that the royalties covered a second month's holiday in the Highlands that year. But 1928 brought a change that cut Alison to the heart. Her uncle James Craw decided to sell Foulden West Mains. "We simply don't think about it. I think it holds the most vivid memories of my life – when I was about eight or nine years old." She went in April to pay the last visit, and noted down the names of the stations (on a line now grass-covered) as if each were a holy bead – Innerleithen, Walkerburn, Galashiels, Melrose, St Boswell's, Gordon, Marchmont, Chirnside. At Foulden there were daffodils and primroses in the grass under the silver-trunked beech trees along the drive. "Uncle James in brown tweeds runs down steps, pleasant and humourous and cool, didn't offer to kiss me." The house smelt of hot water in cans and there was a vase of dusty millers on her dressing-table. "I greet everything my eye falls on and recognizes with a pang of pleasure." Uncle James drove Alison and his two sons over to Oldcambus and parked the car by Dowlaw;* then they walked along the top of the cliff, and she set it all down afterwards for her own re-living. The day was cool, as days are in Berwickshire. "A soft gentle sun, grey-blue sky, light mist at sea through which

* A boy poet, Walter Chisholm, lived and died at Dowlaw in the nineteenth century. He was a pupil of William Cairns at Oldcambus School and William edited Walter's poems after his death.

faintly appears the Bass. As we drop lower towards the sea it gets warmer and more summer-like. All at once Uncle J. points out Fast, far below, a few teeth of ruin on an inconsiderable headland, which has a curious foreshortened effect from above, due partly to the neck of rock which leads to it being hidden." They talked of Margaret Tudor, wife of James IV, whose first night in Scotland was spent there. "She must have thought it the edge of the world. . . . We found seapinks, cowslips, scurvy-grass in the rocks, and saw the pair of peregrines that nest here. A pair has nested here for centuries. One of the Logans took and trained a pair and sent them to the Scottish king. The line of peregrines has outlasted the house of Logan at Fast. The gulls wheeled and cried and rocked on the smooth sea. We saw eider duck, fulmars, cormorants and peregrines. The sea washed pleasantly on the rocks below. One looked like a dragon stretched out to lap the gently swaying sea – only by the light darkening on it could one tell there was a slight swell. Uncle James continually asked the boys names of birds and flowers, reminded them of outings and what they had brought home, told them the names of farms and houses we passed and where the roads led to."

After the charged and undigested travel diary, and the conscious effort of her letters, this Berwickshire page is like the cool thin purling of an underground stream. Above ground 1928 was a year poorer through the departure of Oliver de Selincourt from Aberdeen, a fellow unbeliever whose company had been very welcome, and marked by the sickening of her correspondence with Francis. Her travels and his – for he had started for home in 1927, but stopped in Australia – had interrupted the correspondence, so that in August 1927 Alison had written "Don't disappear please . . . and do write. I feel a very high value in your letters." Francis replied with something more than a letter, for he enclosed some verses begun in 1925 and revised during a great crisis of doubt in 1927, inscribed *To Junia, Asking him how he found the New World*. The verses were sent to revive old memories and test her reaction, and her reply was not altogether discouraging since she wrote "I had truly nearly given you up" and invited him when he returned to join her and

David in a week's walking on the Cairngorms. But eight abrupt monosyllables blinded him for a time to everything else. "Thanks for the poem, it was good fun." For some reason the candour so natural to her was throttled and this was not an occasion on which she could exclaim irritably that he was "much too subtle." Francis was confounded, and as letters then took the best part or two months to travel between the antipodes, the backwash of his resentment was still knocking against Alison's writing table in October 1928. "I didn't like you in your long letter and I did again in your last. Now I see. I had simply stopped being a person to you and was someone, almost unknown, against whom you had a grudge and some retrospective bitterness. It was inevitable. I understand pretty well, and I'm sorry. I hope for our friendship's sake that you will come home before very long, for I don't think we can have much real communication as things are."*

Her twenty-sixth birthday came round a few days after she wrote this, and she was at the height of her beauty. Drummond Young in Edinburgh photographed her with moderate success, but no one painted her portrait. Neither Francis nor anyone else had thought of something "amusing" for her to do, but at the end of the year she made at last the long-desired break and went to Geneva, as a promising place to find work, where her father and she both had friends. Her first comments on the city were a little carping. She found it academic, stiff, too clean – hosed daily by the Fire Brigade. Then largely through her friendship with a Genevese family her heart began to warm to the place. These were the Juillards at Le Château Blanc in Villette, with whom she stayed for a few months, making English conversation with the sons and soon endearing herself to the parents. They found thirty years difference in age no barrier. "Et la paix de l'âme dont Alison était si riche, était contagieuse pour nous." Towards the end of 1929 she became secretary to Dr S. K. Datta of the World Committee of the Y.M.C.A., a friend of her father's, "a subtle, very civilised, sardonic Hindu." He also was writing a book, and Alison again found herself advising, criticising and encouraging. All her life she saw the seamy side of authorship,

* Alison to Francis from Aberdeen, 7 October 1928

51

from the day when as a schoolgirl she walked to the General Post Office in Edinburgh with D. S. Cairns, carrying the parcel containing the manuscript of *The Army and Religion* and observed in her diary "It seems a weight off his chest." Whenever her friends deplored that she did not herself take to writing books she would say with some irritation "You have no idea what it means." But even with the knowledge of what it meant, she might still have become a writer. Something tipped the scale – perhaps something as little as the co-ordination of muscles which makes the holding and use of a pen a pleasure instead of a chore.

Now that the five years in Aberdeen were over – "five very lean kine" – she looked back without bitterness. "Now I don't believe they were so scraggy after all. In constant disagreement with my father and rebelling against my estate (this sounds rather like the Shorter Catechism) yet I learned an immense deal unconsciously from being with him, and now I am always conscious of this. He is you know a very wise and magnanimous person. [Marginal note on magnanimous: 'Used in the widest sense.'] As for the masters – I believe that I've learned more from music (specially Beethoven) than from the poets in these later years, this would make the pure aesthetes howl with disgust." She was writing to Francis. Beethoven illumined D. S. Cairns; they both liked a sombre, dramatic theme and both were giants. "Life opens up surprisingly. The game seems to have rules and that makes it so much more interesting." And the pace of living in Geneva was brisker. She learned to ski, the first sport to give her real pleasure. Through Flora Burley, an Aberdeen friend working in the League secretariat, she met Bess Tapper, and through her the two Deutschman sisters, Marthe and Stefa, Polish girls of great charm and brilliance.* A young Scotswoman, the daughter of a professor of Theology, was not an irresistible draw to those sisters, and it took the determination of Bess to arrange a picnic and bring them together. Then she had nothing more to do but enjoy the triumph. Stefa observed

* Marthe married Hugh Spender, and Stefa, Adrien Tixier, who held offices under de Gaulle during the war, and was the Minister for Home Affairs in France after the Liberation until his premature death in 1946

to Marthe that night that Alison Cairns was no ordinary Ecossaise,* and when D. S. Cairns came to Geneva, it was clear to them that this elderly scholar with the voice of an organ was very far from the conventional pattern of a Scottish theologian.

Many of the expectations of Alison's childhood had never been fulfilled, for what seemed the beginning of a new kind of experience or the first chapter in a delightful sequence, over and again became an isolated memory from which – after too often relishing – even the flavour vanished away, proving nothing but the once-for-allness of life. But in Geneva, in Marthe and Stefa and their friends she found the kind of people whom she had so passionately admired in the Sichel books. Her father and mine would have called them worldly, and certainly they moved far more naturally among the eminent than among humble people. "Fine, decisive, witty," were the words she chose long afterwards to describe Stefa. Through Bess also she came to know about Misia Sert (née Godebska) and the story and character of that footloose European charmer appealed to Alison all her life, as though Misia (who so rarely to me looks more than cosy on the canvases of Bonnard and Renoir and Vuillard, Toulouse-Lautrec or Valloton) had some knowledge that no one else could divulge.

So in Geneva Alison was happy and amused and occupied; and she was in good health too, writing with secure detachment to Francis: "I heard to-day that D. H. Lawrence was dying of consumption above Nice. It's terrible when one remembers what it was for Keats and for Katherine Mansfield. And yet he has lived. Have you read *Sons and Lovers?* there's life there. This has been on my mind all day and yet not to hurt, a kind of stab but not interfering with the beauty and happiness. Is this terribly obtuse? Have you read Keats' Letters and K.M.'s Letters? There's the same sensitiveness and suffering and high spirits and fiery life about them both. I was constantly reminded of Keats when reading Katherine Mansfield." The dictionary has a word for it, cœnaesthesia, the vital perception, the awareness of everything. But in Katherine Mansfield it degenerated to an insomnia of the senses.

* Unconsciously echoing the verdict of Mme Cremer ten years before – "Oui, elle n'est pas une jeune fille quelconque!"

ALISON returned from Geneva each year to share the family holiday in the Highlands, this being a Law of the Medes and Persians, that she and David should be with their father and Aunt Jessie in one of the villages on Speyside or at Spean Bridge or Killin, in deeper retreat from modern life than by this date the Borders could offer. They walked with energy and enterprise. D. S. Cairns eating in the open was less scrupulous about orange peel than his children thought proper, and met their protests blandly. "Mother Nature will take it all to her ample bosom." It was a law (the return to the Highlands) easy to obey, for the childhood sympathy between Alison and David had grown to be a tie of such strength – though unpossessive – the source of so much contentment to them both, that I cannot think of a comparable relationship between brother and sister in history or in fiction. Nothing was more to their taste than great moor and mountain walks – the element of risk, the loneliness, the Wordsworthian encounters with Highland crofters. One summer at Spean Bridge they yielded to the temptation of planning a long outing with return by train, on the last day of all and to catch the last train of the day from Courrour Halt back to Spean Bridge. They went through the glen, Learg nan Leacan Uisge na Leirg, but it was all further than it seemed on the map, all rougher going, and they could not make it, nor could they possibly return the way they had come. David ran ahead of Alison in a wild hope of stopping the express and did receive a friendly wave of the hand from the engine driver, well on his way to Spean Bridge. Then by running another two miles, he reached Courrour Halt before it closed for the night and was able to telegraph for a taxi to meet them at midnight at the nearest roadhead, the lower end of Loch Treig. Meanwhile Alison waited in the cottage of the

54

signalman at Lochtreighead, helping a little girl who had returned from school with "Tell the stories of all Christ's miracles" as her homework that night. Then they set off, striding awkwardly on the sleepers down the railway line on the steep slope above the haunted waters of the loch; a long dark walk it was. The light in another signalman's cottage made them pause and knock, and when the door was opened there sat a little company playing cards in great formality, the women dressed in the fashion of fifty years earlier with high boned collars to their silk blouses. About midnight they reached their rendez-vous, thankful to see the lights of the car shining on the pitchy mountainsides, as it wound up the road to rescue them.

Dr Datta returned to India in the summer of 1932 and Alison was promised a place on the staff of a new periodical to be published in Geneva for the duration of the Disarmament Conference, but she lost this coveted start in journalism by returning to Scotland for the family holiday at Newtonmore. For some reason she could not take the chance of picking up work in Geneva, and was set for another winter in Aberdeen with nothing better ahead than compiling a survey of Social Work among Adolescent Girls. In her pursuit of an occupation, the sine qua non of an unmarried woman, Alison never fell lower than this, a work on work, almost as silly as all those books about books that clog the arteries of literature. She needed the self-confidence of Bernard Berenson, who believed that by doing less than most people, far less than he could have done, he became more of a work of art himself; but she did, like Berenson, come to "radiate authority and influence" unearned by any achievements that could be listed in an obituary notice. She quoted with relish and I heard with satisfaction the saying of Bishop Mandell Creighton, the father of Gemma Bailey, whom Alison loved so dearly – "Nobody does so much harm as the person who goes about doing good." But back of it all we remained puzzled and uncertain; when and for how long it is justifiable to sport one's oak is not a question any man can answer.

However, soon after Alison settled down to this dismal survey under the auspices of the Scottish Association of Girls' Clubs "at request of and financed by Carnegie Trust," she accepted an invitation to join the staff of the Student Movement House in Russell Square, as sub-warden to Mary Trevelyan – congenial work under a stimulating leader, the right work but not in the right place. She hated London, missed the mountains of Scotland and the mountains of Switzerland, was oppressed by the vastness of the metropolis and more still by a feeling that the devil was gaining ground there. Francis, who had returned from the antipodes in 1931 and visited her in Geneva, was now in London too, making up fast for the years of exile, pleased to entertain Alison and introduce her to his friends, pleased to go to her parties; but not in an easy mood. He could no longer bring himself to use any magic word in the faint hope that it would bring out of the heavens the moment of rapprochement.

The following winter a great fatigue began to trouble her, which she put down to the poisonous air of London and lack of exercise. With the mixture of ignorance and discipline that regulated her physical life, she took up rowing on the Serpentine. The result was a pain in her chest which she supposed to be muscular. She paid little attention to it, but tried to understand what had gone wrong in her dealings with people, and why she felt so inadequate. At the peak of this dissatisfaction the doctors also looked within her and were dissatisfied, and responsibility was shifted to their shoulders. Her lungs were X-rayed after an attack of pleurisy in the early summer of 1935, and a spot was found on one of them. The information that she had pulmonary tuberculosis was passed to her in a restaurant.

D. S. Cairns' threatened chest trouble more than forty years earlier had given him a fruitful winter in Egypt and he hoped that Alison too would benefit by rest and change and time to think. Another aspect, however, worried him. "You realize," he said to David, "this will affect her prospects of marriage." Alison had taken the news "quite straight," as Priscilla Clark* (with whom she shared a flat) observed, and "neither hid her dismay nor made anything of it," as indeed she took all the misfortunes and disappointments of life. The pretence of health,

* Priscilla, daughter of Roger and Sarah Clark of Street, had been at the Mount with Alison

although she had not realized it was a pretence, was thankfully dropped, and she entered Brompton Hospital in the middle of July 1935. Three weeks later, already feeling better, she wrote me at length.*

"I feel very fraudulent, sitting here, temperature normal, steadily putting on weight, having no treatment but rest and large meals. At times it seems that all this time and leisure is a free gift – one sinks into oneself, pulls out one's thoughts and has a look at them, discovers what one really thinks about a number of things, and does quite a lot of mental and emotional disentangling – all this of course is absorbing – then there are times of utmost tedium – 'I want to play golf and I don't want to play golf, what shall I do Mummy?' You remember Letty's story.

"*The Decline and Fall* is unsurpassed for sending one to sleep in the middle of the day – those terrific sentences weigh down the eyelids in a most agreeable fashion. Between 6 and 7 p.m. however they have another effect. Why should the account of the formation of the Legions in battle and on the march be so interesting, and the sense one has of the range of empire? Shut up here in rather a dark corner it's like looking out of a window at a stupendous view. And I find the Wall continually in my mental pictures, and Borcovicus that thundery summer evening.

"I had one of your mother's best letters the other day – how I like the way her writing and indeed her style swings across the page. I know so well your feeling of having a 'permanent lease' of the Albany Mansions flat.† When Foulden was sold I had a feeling of immense melancholy about it until I realised that my memories of it were so vivid that it was always there for me to walk about, through the rooms and in the orchard and garden. Indeed it has been one of my amusements here – and the strangest things come back – for instance sitting in the wagonette

* The previous December, 1934, I had married Max Newman, the mathematician, a Fellow of St John's College, Cambridge, and we were living in Peter Kapitza's house in Cambridge, on the point of moving into an old farmhouse at Comberton, five miles out. This is the Cross Farm which Alison mentions in a number of her letters. It was Max and I whom she named when Priscilla Clark said "But which of our friends has married a man of her own calibre I would like to know."

† The flat I rented in Battersea from 1927 to 1934, where Alison frequently stayed with me

just starting for church, how one would *hear* the horses' hooves start and *then*, a fraction of a second later, when the harness or trappings or whatever they were, were taut, how the carriage started. I have started going round the place in my memory and so far have got no further than the back yard and kitchen – haven't begun to go up the kitchen stairs yet! – and most unexpected of all, I find I can remember smells – or at any rate the kind of feeling that accompanies particular smells. It's all a kind of physical memory that is peculiarly rich and satisfactory.

"Did I mention *A Life of One's Own* by Joanna Field to you? It's a rather solemnly written account by a woman psychologist of the mental or rather psychological technique she evolved for herself. Much of it is rather obvious and she has this very tiresome solemn style, but what has interested me is her account of a certain kind of seeing – sometimes natural scenery, sometimes chairs and tables. Have you ever had it? – as if scales had fallen from the eyes – as if one were looking at the final, the complete chair – the most heavenly experience suddenly falling on one from nowhere. I have it sometimes. J. F. maintains she can command this type of seeing by an appropriate mental gesture, but I have never been able to. Oddly enough I've never discovered any one who has had this experience – though it must be common enough, probably to you yourself."

The day before her thirty-third birthday, 17 October 1935, Alison was transferred to the King Edward VII Hospital at Midhurst, just three days before I was confined; and on 31 October she wrote:

"I was so pleased to get your letter an hour ago that instead of putting it among the 50 (yes, literally) that await answers, I feel I must talk to you straight away. I can hardly believe that all this happened to you only ten days ago, and that you should so soon be doing such normal things as writing letters. Those of us who are not mothers, I suppose, think of delivery as a grave, terrifying and dangerous event – which it is – but into which the mother is caught and wrapped and held for an immense period. Poor Edward, what a birth – my sympathy would normally be for you, but yours I see is all for him.

"My latest interest has been falling in love in a way I never supposed I should again, i.e. quite irresponsibly and with very little knowledge or appreciation of the man. It was simply an amusing flirtation that gained on me imperceptibly. There was some stress and strain as you can imagine about being in this state in hospital, but now that I have left the object of my affections in London – and the probabilities are that the affair stops here – I can afford to be pleased to know that I can still entertain such feelings. I had thought that middle age was upon me. Incidentally I believe that t.b. rather tends to heighten natural amorousness. Hence the peculiar and stringent rules of this sanatorium where we are forbidden to walk in mixed bands. At evening concerts men and women may mingle, but not when a film is shown. So far I have only been allowed to get up for tea, but to-day have permission to go downstairs for both lunch and tea. This tiresome very slight temperature persists, rather puzzling the doctors I gather, for they assure me there is very little trouble indeed in my lung, and my weight increases alarmingly. I am now positively blousy. I feel I need hardly be here, and yet at Brompton had before me so many tragic examples of people who had not stopped the thing in time, and I took the doctor's advice in a very docile way.

"A letter from home tells me that my father's aunt has died at the age of 96. Poor old dear, she had been very wandery for some time. Among the better of her wanderings was the conviction that my good and delightful Uncle Willie was bigamously married to a publican's daughter. She is to be buried to-morrow at Biggar. She was born in the manse described in the Letter to Dr John Cairns. Dr John's* father, whose wife died there, was her uncle, her mother's brother, so you see to us she is a link with quite another world. Her mother lived to be 100 – all but a few months, and I think dominated her completely, so that she only came into her own life at the age of 70. Several suitors I believe were dismissed so that she might remain with 'mamma.' Mamma was always spoken of in a reverential voice, so that about 2 years ago when she was staying at Braidburn Crescent and I was sitting in the same room, I was startled to hear a

* John *Brown*, M.D. Author of *Horæ Subsecivæ*, in the second series of which the "Letter to Dr John Cairns" appeared

quavery voice remark to itself 'Of course I always did like papa better than mamma.' "*

An account of the funeral at Biggar was sent by David and gave Alison as great pleasure as her letter had given me a week earlier. "Two hearts positively that beat as one, for I would see and feel it all exactly as you described it – the elderlies, the sense of mortality, the repressed tiff with Aunt K. The parent and uncle, top-hatted and bouncing and incredibly dear and pathetic – pathetic only because they are mortal, as you and I may be now, or shall be anyway."† Nonsense of course, for the arrows of death cut the air around all of us day and night, but she still nursed the youthful illusion that death for herself and her contemporaries might be indefinitely retarded, and for many of Alison's family and of mine too, old age proved to be a tranquil journey to natural euthanasia, in the fashion of Great-uncle John, protesting shortly before he died that he did not feel at all ill.

* Alison to Lyn from Midhurst 31 October 1935

† Alison to David from Midhurst 12 November 1935. The funeral party was driven to Biggar in one of "the big, bouncy Daimlers beloved of undertakers."

MOST OF her life Alison had neither the time nor the disposition to keep a journal. She picked the best out of the day for conversation or a letter and let the rest go, except on a few occasions when she felt compelled to unburden her heart in her *Shriek Book*. It was more than private; she even sealed some of the pages together to discourage herself from re-reading them. As she prepared to leave Midhurst in March 1936 she wrote in the book "This going north now, about the most difficult thing I have had to face." Horribly teased by memories of her abortive affair at Brompton, she felt the current of life running very strong against her, but she did not look for happiness or forgetfulness, only "I must believe, I must believe, I *must believe* that some living principle will emerge." So austere, she was, so diffident, not asking for faith larger than a grain of mustard seed.

She made a long and careful investigation of her need to smoke – for she had been a heavy smoker even in Geneva, and left the Juillards' house in order to have a room to sleep in and another to smoke in. Then *not* smoking – it had given her "tremendous moral kick – one could push down a house," and she remembered after stopping in 1934 how "bright ideas and illuminations came into my mind over a period of about a week – quite unsought for." For nine days she smoked rather less. Then she returned to Joanna Field for help, to a second book *An Experiment in Leisure*. "J.F.'s theory about things that you like, that seem to touch you in some deep region of yourself. For her, horned creatures, subterranean fires. For me trees: on the golf course at Killin on a September morning. In the streets of Tübingen early on a May morning as D. and I set out for Vienna. The birch tree in the sun on the moor at Rothiemurchus, when there in 1934 with David, Mary and Chat Vail – they

61

went on and left me. Rivers with rather small streams – that little stream at Diablerets in the summer of 1923. Was my love and attitude almost of worship for them – the feeling that at least they were deeply important – an indication that unconsciously I wanted to be in touch with what J.F. calls 'the force by which one is lived.' I have never felt this, never – that's why I am so unreligious I suppose. I was always in the saddle and responsible, is that what makes experience seem thin most of the time?"

In the saddle, and judging herself without pity or understanding, not seeing the tree that she herself had become.

> Mein Leben ist nicht diese steile Stunde
> darin du mich so eilen siehst
> Ich bin ein Baum vor meinem Hintergrunde.*

But as she sat within the unloved walls of 139 Desswood Place, waiting for something to break the tedium of her convalescence, she was pleased to note that her negative attitude towards marriage – amounting to nothing much more than an idea that a woman who doesn't marry has failed – had given place to something better, a need to give and a desire to receive. So she wrote to me in 1936: "I quite suddenly feel ready to be married – not faute de mieux, but a curious psychological change. There are no men in Scotland, such a pity. I think I should like to marry an intelligent coloured tough, preferably with a streak of Jew in him." Someone quite unlike a Cairns or a Craw – it was a sound impulse. But she always insisted upon intelligence and culture, and when any woman brought up as she had been, married into a poor or illiterate family, she viewed the alliance with amazement – "the kind of marriage I can't believe."

D. S. Cairns' Baird Lectures (of 1932) had never been prepared for the press and Alison now saw as her most obvious duty to "joggle" him till it was done, and the only way that she could achieve this, to come to grips herself with the material; which she did with so much success – in spite of her distaste for theology – that the lectures appeared in 1937, under the title *The Riddle of the World*.

---

* Rainer Maria Rilke, *Book of Hours*. (As for my life, it isn't this headlong descent that you see. I am a tree, standing before my background.)

"I am having a very quiet life here, taking a daily constitutional down Union Street and trying to immerse myself in the Bairds. Spirits I am thankful to say are tolerably good. No more has *transpired* about the post I covet, but one or two hints have been vouchsafed by Fergusson and Tom which makes me hope. Also the Principal, dear, in speaking to Pa, referred to me by my first name, though our acquaintance is but slight. However I'm not really thinking about it, it's only in the background of the mind, potent as a cheering possibility. If it does not come off, it will have served its purpose as such." So she wrote to David on 28 October 1936. To me on December 18 the same year:

"My future is wrop in mystery and sometimes I think gloom, but that is a line one mustn't allow oneself to take. Physically I am extremely well and the doctors tell me I can do anything . . . in reason they add. But when I asked, as a kind of test, how long I could safely overwork, my little chest-man replied 'About a year I should say.' Quite a good margin! – not that I propose to put it to the test."

After forty-five years in the ministry, twenty-eight at Aberdeen, my father was about to retire, and he discussed his plans with D. S. Cairns, who came down strongly against moving from Aberdeen, for a reason which had never entered my father's head and struck him as very odd and amusing. "Man, if you stay here, think what a funeral they'll give you!" The memory of the phalanx of mourners, from the West End to the top of the Mound, following Great-uncle John to his grave, was still potent enough to bamboozle the nephew for a moment. But my father, able to forego this posthumous delight, chose to live in a house in Biggar, a stone's throw from the manse where Alison's great-grandparents had lived and her great-aunt Nancy had been born.

"My father and I have just been having a farewell tea at Westfield Terrace – that well-liked house. I was sad to be there for the last time, but not too sad, for one never really loses places. Your mother was in splendid spirits and told me one of her stories about a missionary meeting in Craigiebuckler Church. Your father had just come, with mine, from burying Miss

63

Abernethy. . . . [Alison's punctuation. She knew that I would appreciate the decorum of a pause after that august name.] Your mother was as pleased as a child about the £33 wireless set, the field glasses and the sapphire necklet,* and talked about the Daphne Mesereum and the Azaleas that she had bought for the Biggar garden.† But about the King [Edward, Duke of Windsor] 'he will probably kill himself and that might be the best thing that could happen to him' – so lugubriously that we all burst out laughing."§

Francis had written to Alison in June 1936, soon after she left Midhurst, and on December 14 of that year she sat down to answer his letter.

"I am sorry about La Rochefoucauld and that you can never forgive me. . . . a long pause here for a cigarette while I consider and come to the conclusion that I don't really know what forgiveness is. Either one accepts people and forgiveness becomes irrelevant, or one doesn't and forgiveness is a kind of armistice, but not the noble generous thing people make it out to be. However it has such a standing as an act of virtue that I am ready to suppose that it's some defect in me or incompleteness of experience that keeps me from seeing it. Forgive me, how heavy and pedantic. Take those remarks please as general considerations – which is indeed what they are, and not as comments on your comments, which made me feel a pig, but I am sorry I really couldn't help being a confused pig sixteen – mon Dieu! – years ago – sometimes I can't help it even now."

He replied at once (as she might have foreseen) asking her to come and stay with him in Shropshire, but she was expecting to go to London in a few weeks and to Somerset at Easter, "and my pocket won't stand three journeys abroad (for that's what it amounts to) in four months." However it was arranged that she should go there on her way back from Somerset. She wrote to me blithely about the visit – how much she had enjoyed Francis' mother, who had looked at Alison "with a question mark in her eye." To Francis himself she wrote:

* Presents from the congregation
† None of these survived the winter climate of Biggar
§ Alison to Lyn from Aberdeen, 12 December 1936

64

"Never have I enjoyed more delightful hospitality, I did enjoy seeing you established with so much that you have always wanted. No circumstances could be pleasanter, 35 schools to build in the teeth of the clergy and those heavenly country evenings to come back to. Beware the visionary creeping moss. This isn't really an impertinent counsel but a very beautiful line of poetry which I seem to have composed, and which as it is likely to remain a fragment, must be written down.

"It was a very great pleasure to meet your mother. Do tell me if you ever go and see old Uncle Hill again. I don't expect he will live long. I think that what I like about truly religious people is that their centre is outside of themselves and that seems to give them a freshness and vitality that is very fine. Perhaps this in itself is true religion, I don't know."

Besides the matter of expense in December and January that winter, Alison had another reason for staying at home. The retirement of her father – at seventy-four – was giving them both food for much discussion, making and un-making of plans, "titanic inward swithers." When Alison had only herself to consider, swithering held no fascination, but now sympathy and love obliged her to shoulder each indecision as it rose. David also was in some perplexity and she wrote to him regretting that she was too biased to give advice.* "If I said that the more agreeable course is not necessarily the wrong course as we with our scrupulosity always tend to think, I fear you would see me simply as a snake twining round an apple tree. Whichever decision you take I don't suppose God will abandon you – I wonder if this is a subconscious fear."

Alison herself had been put on the short list of the National Peace Council in London for a post at the salary of £264 a year. Their solicitor in Aberdeen, James Fraser, at first advised her to go ahead – he "took the line that I must consider my life, that it was a crucial decision at my age, but later after talk rather arrived at the point of view I had been tending towards," namely that her father should retire in 1937 and the Aberdeen

---

* David's footnote to this: "I was already in a charge, and had only been a short time in it – this was a letter from the Principal of one of the Scottish Universities asking if I would stand for a chair"

house be sold and another bought in Edinburgh, and Alison postpone taking any work until all this was accomplished. "I was much shaken by other considerations. This was a chance to get back to London, work, and my own generation, which might not come again – that as you may imagine is a thought that makes my craven spirit quail." After it had all been settled – Alison not to go for her interview, D. S. Cairns to retire – that same evening he became restive and announced that he would go and talk to James Fraser. Alison, afraid that he had changed his mind, went with him, for "after arriving at a decision, and with a limited time to act, one just can't reopen considerations and go through the whole harrowing process again." But after an hour she was sent home by her father and went to bed with a book. "At 1 a.m. in comes Pa. Sees the light under my door comes in very fresh and brisk and smiling. 'I have made up my mind. I am not going to retire this year. But,' said he, 'I am not going to discuss it any further to-night.' "* The following morning Alison left for London, but she was *not* offered the post with the National Peace Council. So the date for retirement might be further argued. "I am very glad, to let the whole matter rest for the moment." It was now the end of January and wild weather. "Yesterday Margaret Fyfe and I went down to have a look at the sea – it was magnificent – white breakers as far as the eye could see, and great waves crashing on the beach. We went along the south end of the esplanade and watched a German trawler struggle in to the harbour – then we ran (in her car) down to the harbour and watched it slip in, 'port after stormy seas.' The men came up quite unconcerned from down below and in a minute the swastika ran up the mast. This morning flags were up at the end of each breakwater showing that no boat should come in, and the trawlers were all lying tossing outside."

When the further argument about their future plans took place, D. S. Cairns reverted to the idea of retiring in 1937, so Alison made a number of visits to Edinburgh and found three suitable houses for him to inspect. This had an adverse effect; inward swithering set in again, in the middle of which he went

* Alison to David from Aberdeen, 27 January 1937

66

to his doctor "about a small matter that had been troubling him and was ordered into a nursing home at once for a very minor operation. The doctors told him it was nothing, but told me it was almost certainly cancer. But it wasn't. *Broke are their nets and thus escaped we.* All this you can imagine has been harrowing."* But the illness though slight brought him to the point of deciding to retire that summer. All the three houses had been snapped up by other buyers, but Alison started again and found 13 Mayfield Terrace. Before moving she drew breath and came to stay with us at Cross Farm for a week, returning on June 2 to "the cold Edinburgh rain, mourning for my dear friends, and the sun and the buttercups. I'm still partly with you, though the bodily A.H.C. has been measuring floors and windows for carpets and curtains all afternoon. I found my aunt well, but very old. She sends you her love. When she heard of the Rev. Mr Jardine speeding to bless the union of Edward and Mrs S. she folded her hands and said 'This must be a *great* comfort to Queen Mary.' "

We had lent her Karin Stephen's *Psychoanalysis and Medicine* to read on the long journey home by train and her comment was "Interesting, but Freudian analysis is dull, anything can mean anything and its opposite as well. What can the mind do with that, the practising analyst perhaps can, because he's using more than his mind. And I can't feel that all neuroses have their primary causes in infantile sexual frustration, lots of them have, but why erect it into a permanent exclusive truth. Just like the theologians again.

"I did so much enjoy that week with you. Do you find that pleasant, particularly pleasant times resolve themselves for you into a key picture that acts as a sort of symbol for the rest, the first thing that you lay the fingers of your mind on – mine that week is standing late one evening with you, leaning on the gate at the foot of the garden, talking about the reproductive habits of cats."† A very still and lovely May evening it was, and stories of our fastidious and faithful tabby amused Alison. We gazed over the gate down the meadow, to where the seamless

* Alison to Lyn from Aberdeen 6 May 1937. The quotation was a favourite of Alison's; it comes from the seventh verse of the second version of Psalm 124 in the Scottish Psalter.

† Alison to Lyn from Aberdeen, 18 July 1937

67

carpet of buttercups had vanished beneath a quilt of mist. "How strange," said Alison, "that after those choppy years in London, you should now be settled in this peaceful place." I heard the words uneasily – settled – peaceful – with Hitler in power in Germany! This visit turned out to be her last to Cross Farm for thirteen years. Without knowing that we must make the most of it, yet we did, and several remarks of Alison's are as audible still in my memory as if she had said them only a few days ago. Max had expressed surprise at Alison's pleasure in meeting a village friend, to me a very dear friend. "But Alison, she has the brain of a hen." "That may well be! But if she found herself vicereine of India to-morrow, she'd know exactly how to behave." And whenever Alison asserted her opinion against the narrowness of the academic, her eyes blazed with a particular brightness. Some drollery of Max's set her laughing another day – made in parting as he put us down in St Andrew's Street in Cambridge. We laughed for some minutes as we walked along and then Alison drew breath and said to me cryptically, but with great emphasis: "I can forgive a man anything if he makes me laugh." But Alison, who could laugh at almost anything until her sides ached when she was sixteen, and was just as eager to be amused at thirty or forty or fifty, found her entertainment always further to seek. And each year she took more trouble to amuse others. I would not call her a wit, but she was a good raconteuse with a gift for mimicry. In an Edinburgh tram one day Lord and Lady Beveridge attracted the attention of the woman sitting next to Alison. "Verra foand" she whispered with a nudge and wink, and Alison was delighted to whisper back that it was Lord Beveridge and his lady, and observe the impression. "Whit a brain!" She played all this back to the Beveridges the first time that she met them, with great success.

All June 1937 and part of July Alison spent going back and forwards between Aberdeen and Edinburgh, preparing the one house to be emptied and the other to be filled, and making her farewells in Aberdeen. "David and I have succeeded at last in parting with our rocking horse and the parent has succeeded in parting with very little indeed, to my despair. I cannot believe that we are actually leaving Aberdeen, and have been too busy to discover if I mind much or not. I think I feel more strongly that something is beginning than that something is ending. Our old life in Aberdeen, you and I walking up and down Westfield Terrace, David and I looking after our gardens in Rubislaw Terrace or going on bicycling expeditions with the Forgans, came to an end so long ago, that it all might have happened in another place. This last winter has been pleasant and I leave seven or eight people with real regret, but d'you know I believe Geneva is the place I return to with all the sentiments people are alleged to have about their homes, almost 'thy very stones to me are dear.' "

This letter of 18 July was the last that she wrote to me from 139 Desswood Place. I must quote the whole of it for full measure.

"You saw Letty* didn't you? I saw her twice in Edinburgh, and then at the Shetland boat here with Helmut and Christopher. They looked so beautifully cosmopolitan among the other passengers, hearty ladies with rucksacks, men going up to fish, a few commercial travellers. Helmut was certain he would be very sea sick and read in guttural Italian from the boat to us on the quay the instructions for taking a new seasick cure. I liked him instantly, mainly because I like another Austrian Jew whom he slightly resembled. What an engaging, disarming creature Letty is. I am sorry to be leaving Margaret and Rex† – he has been extremely kind in giving time and advice to, and about a neurotic friend of mine here, and at a time when he was particularly busy. He displayed real kindness and sympathy and a good deal of insight. I also like his warm and slightly flirtatious manner – it cheers me very much in a world of – ——s [mentioning Aberdeen's most eligible and least susceptible bachelor]. I think he and Margaret should be good for each other. What an odious thing to say – too reminiscent of a question my father asks David and myself to our fury, about our friends 'Has so-and-so *developed*?'

"By the way next time you are in Edinburgh you must see a

* Letty, *née* Grierson, the fourth daughter of Sir Herbert, married then to Helmut Lehmann-Haupt

† Knight. Rex was Professor of Psychology and had recently married Margaret Horsey a contemporary of ours at Girton.

very charming little picture my aunt has of Lady Waterford and her sister – not reproduced in *Two Noble Lives* which she also possesses and which I mean to borrow. The original of the picture – a crayon of two beautiful heads – was picked up by a Kelso photographer at a sale of furniture in a 'big house.' He framed it and put it in his window and not long after a surprised visitor to Kelso entered his shop and asked him how he had come into possession of this portrait of his two aunts. The photographer sold him the picture, but first had it photographed, and sold copies framed – one to my grandmother who was interested in the painter of the scripture pictures in the school at Ford (Lady Waterford).

"Coming up with my father along Carden Place today we met Miss Galloway – do you remember a rather inept lady I used to bully disgustingly in the French class? She is plump and pink and comfortable-looking now. She told me that Miss Middleton is dead. Did you know? That gave me quite a pang. I used to think her a wonderful person, such élan, such style, such spirit, and I used to think so romantic with that dark face and large nose. So masterful she was too – I can't remember anything she taught us but she was never dull. I am *sorry* she is dead – and Miss Bower too, Miss Galloway said. Only she and Miss Grant and Miss Niven are left of these people.*

"I must stop, a thousand loathsome duties call. Do write me soon. What did Edward say or look when he saw the sea? My love to Max. And very much to yourself.

Alison

My father, as we returned from the Graduation Reception last week remarked absently 'They don't seem to be doing as many of these *dog* trots as they used to, do they?' "†

From the very start she felt at home in Edinburgh and liked the new house. It was "ordinary enough" but gave her a pleasant feeling, and every time that she went out, no matter how prosaic her errand, the city gave her a shock of delight. "So dramatic, so romantic – even coming out here on the tram one glances down grey side streets to see the sun on Salisbury

---

* Teachers at Mr Mackie's School when Alison and I were there
† Alison to Lyn from Aberdeen 18 July 1937

Crags, or Arthur's Seat heaving up like a mountain. Princes Street is full of American lovelies just now, and Scotland does not feel like a backwater! My parent is pleased to think he looks on the back of the houses of Spence Street, where his uncle John lived, and just round the corner from us is Arthur Lodge where Dr John Brown's father lived and my grandmother, his niece, kept house for him when she was a girl. So I suppose it's some atavistic feeling that makes me feel at home here! Later on it may become very oppressive, but at the moment I feel at home as never in Aberdeen."*

* Alison to Lyn from Edinburgh, 1 August 1937

ON THE quay at Toulon, early in 1938, Alison stood with her father waiting to embark on one of the Hellenic Cruises, scanning the other passengers doubtfully. It would have been folly to refuse a chance to see Greece and the Holy Land, but "foreseeing the company as composed mainly of bishops and retired clergy, I had no pleasant expectations.... my only thought was 'Nothing now remains except to behave well.'" In fact this journey was happy and memorable and her fellow-travellers not so homogeneous as she feared. She had not foreseen such gratifications as being sought out after a dance by a Jesuit priest who had observed and remembered each of her partners and wished to discuss them with her. (Did he hope that *his* church would not have turned a blind eye to her gifts, the fruit of thirteen centuries of Border Christianity, less than half of it Protestant?)

"It's nonsense to say Jerusalem has been spoiled. One has the impression of looking at the Crusaders' city. I had introductions to influential Jews and Arabs and we went out a lot socially to Zionist parties and visits to Sheiks. The tension is fierce and both sides seem equally implacable. It is fantastic to think that this apparently insoluble problem was gratuitously created by us twenty years ago – of course it has been very much exacerbated by European Anti-Semitism. Our Arab friends were charming gentle, intelligent people, fine in the grain, but one felt they didn't stand a chance against the Jews – American and German mostly we met, tough, brilliant, vital creatures, as arrogant and exclusive as the Children of Israel, for the second time taking possession of the promised land.

"Our fellow-passengers were mixed, some notables, among whom the Alingtons and the Inges were the most interesting, and every kind of clergyman from nice Dr Mackinnon, parish

THE REVEREND PRINCIPAL
D. S. CAIRNS D.D.

minister of Kilmonivaig, above Fort William, to Father D'Arcy, England's most brilliant Jesuit and our chief charmer, whose celibacy I can only deplore. The average age, the purser told me was 65, and we had a number of lame old army men and deaf old peers, among whom old Ld Polwarth was alternatively my responsibility – and when I evaded it – my reproach, as owing to my piercing voice I was the only person he could hold sustained converse with.

"Dearest Lyn – I *have* written you a travel letter after all but it was all such fun I am still carried away when I think of it. And you would have enjoyed my father's pleasure. I don't think I have ever seen him enjoy anything so much. I wish you could have seen him skipping up and down the walls of Jerusalem."*

After the Hellenic Cruise she gradually gave up the struggle to remain outside the church. In pencil on a loose piece of paper she examined her conversion.

"How shall I explain this change from diffidence often increasing to antagonism into an emotional assent to the Xtian story and a feeling I would rather be inside the Xtian church than outside?

"Going to Palestine I had no expectations of interest, had formed no mental pictures of what I would find there – was regarding the whole thing as anyway a temporary escape possibly, but not very likely offering possibility of a permanent escape (marriage) from a way of living that seemed to hold no more possibilities and no prospects of security in the future. Arrived at Haifa in the rain, the oil pipe line from Iraq and the brook Kedron. Then we drove through that green hilly country Galilee. F., K.M.B.† and me. I was deeply moved – tags of poetry кept sounding in my mind. 'O fair green hills of Galilee.' 'Thou has conquered O pale Galilean.' 'And did those feet in ancient time. . . .' Hole's pictures familiar since we were very small and Sunday evenings with Father – I think had something to do with the mood. F. and K.M.B. too felt it strongly – there was a unity of feeling that quite swept away all the irritation I

---

* Alison to Lyn from Birling Gap, Eastbourne, 26 April 1938
† Kathleen Morrison-Bell

so often feel. Then later in the day we drove along the shores of
the Lake – a grey and luminous day. Looking across to the
mountains of Gadara. 'It was here, it was here, it was here' –
something long familiar had become *actualised*. One wasn't in a
keyed up state of exultation all the time – which would have
simply brought a reaction. There was the episode of F. going
for a holy sail with a band of Xtians and coming off in a fury
because of Punch and his questions – also the Arab children with
flowers and shell necklaces. Coming back along the Lake F.
stopped our car above the supposed site of Capernaum, and got
out and stood and looked for a long time and said: 'It was here
he lived and taught most of his 3 years.' And I thought of F.
and his long life, 75 years, following and teaching the truths of
that life of 2000 years ago, and here at the end of it he had come
to the place where it had actually happened, an old man."

The massive pronouncements of her teaching and preaching
ancestry were now broken down into the vernacular of places,
people, the sky, flowers, weather – the vernacular which Jesus
Christ himself had used. When Alison found she could accept
the faith into which she had been baptized, it was not by change
of heart bringing a change of life. For like Lord Hermand at the
General Assembly of 1805, she could truly have said "Sir! I
sucked in the being and attributes of God with my mother's
milk." Rather something that she had never denied – never
could deny – became so alive to her that the trappings of church
membership no longer offended. This I believe was true, and
yet she once said to me "You know, I had to travel a long way
from the beliefs of my family and do things that would have
horrified them, before I could make my reconciliation."

Soon after their return from the Hellenic Cruise, Alison went
for some months to Birling Gap, near Eastbourne, to help Dr
Stanton Coit of the Ethical Church to write his memoirs. The
old man was bored with the task, and although Alison now had
considerable experience of encouraging the unwilling author,
the work led nowhere. Alison did not even discover until 1954
that as a boy Stanton Coit had seen Abraham Lincoln assas-
sinated. When she spent a weekend in London she noted the
"very jittery atmosphere over these German Czech frontier

74

incidents. As one of the papers pointed out, Hitler personally in a moment of unbalanced rage over one of these reported incidents might set the whole thing going." Alison stayed, actually slept, at the Ethical Church, sharing the vestry with a large gold bust of Josephine Butler, and attended a service in the church the next morning. After Shelley's *Ode to the West Wind* magnificently sung in the Gregorian mode, "most of the hymns were about the Right, and cheer up, for Right always wins in the end 'Say not the struggle naught availeth' and so on. Rather pathetic in a way I thought. There were no prayers. I walked across Hampstead Heath to supper with Priscilla and her parents who were staying with her. It was a superb evening and the Heath looked like the Elysian fields, freshest green, a golden light on the trees, the grass, and the ponds, and the Sunday crowds walked like the blessed in glory, a mediaeval picture, you know what I mean, boys and girls arm in arm, little dogs skipping round, lots of detail. Physically the time at Birling Gap has been very profitable for I feel fine, have put on 3 or 4 lbs in weight, have done some stiff reading, some German, some thinking, some meditating!"*

In July of this year, Jessie Cairns died, at 20 Braidburn Crescent. "Your letter about Aunt Jaye brought her essential nature so clearly into my mind. In her life she made so few claims, was so unostentatious, so unselfconscious, that we, or I rather, took her for granted. Now one recognizes her quality and that there was nothing second-rate about her. She had such a fresh warm interest in people and had a huge correspondence. We used to laugh at her for her interminable letter-writing. The other day in Braidburn Crescent I picked up one of her little pocket diaries for 1933 or 1934, and I found in the blank memorandum pages at the end she had copied: 'A letter can be begun or ended as the mood dictates, written in a sickroom or in a crowd of company, and the inspiration is given and renewed perpetually by the demands of friendship and the desire to give pleasure where one loves.'†

"We are all so thankful she got away so easily. She suddenly

* Alison to David from Birling Gap 24 May 1938
† Quoting from my first book *Ten Letter Writers*. Hogarth Press 1932.

became very weak on the afternoon of the 26th. Joan helped her into bed, she protesting and laughing characteristically at her own helplessness. Then she gradually became unconscious and died in her sleep next morning. Your father and mother came to see us on Wednesday, such a pleasure. . . . Lyn what a *queer* thing death is, unimaginably strange when one sees it."*

The next few months she was busy in a way that became very familiar to her. "For a long time at B.B.C. I really enjoyed being there and going through Aunt Jaye's things, for one felt so strongly as if she was still there in the house and enjoying our interest. But now the place is half dismantled and a 'For Sale' board at the gate, and we shall be glad to be finished. My dear the papers, about 100 years of letters, and some of them interesting so that we can't destroy wholesale. My uncle is a sensible fellow, reads and tears, but the parent has too much sensibility, reads and lays on one side 'to be decided on later.' Bales come back here and letters of 1843 mingle with the morning's post. I decided a week ago not to lose my temper again but to regard it all as a discipline and a hair shirt.

"I was out at Biggar a short time ago seeing the Pairmans. I visited your mother and she told me about Geoffrey's death.† I was so very sorry to hear of it, and remembered that you had given me a sad account of him in July. You will miss him much, and Yda must feel that a pillar has gone. When you spoke of him I always remembered him, not as I saw him latterly once or twice, but that evening years ago in your flat, do you remember, when he read Shakespeare to us – Henry IV wasn't it – and his enthusiasm, like a young man's, or something younger, like you and me reading Tennyson to each other in Aberdeen. 'Isn't this bit lovely?'

"I felt like writing to you during the Crisis, but what could one do but exclaim. Everything that happened before then

* Alison to Lyn from Edinburgh, 6 August 1938
† Geoffrey Marks (1864–1938), well-known in actuarial circles, a founder-member of the esoteric Tuesday Club (which dined on Wednesdays), first-nighter, bibliophile. I suppose that he was a remarkable and sometimes alarming person, but "I *know* he was my kind dear friend," and his enthusiasms endeared him to many others. He met Ellen Terry for the first time when they were both middle-aged and said "Ma'am, I saw you play Juliet when I was a boy in my teens." "Did you?" she said in her lovely husky voice. "Did you like me?" "I would have died for you."

seems months ago. It was a queer time and there are queer times ahead. Chamberlain did save us from war (if only he hadn't said Peace with honour) but his judgment has been belied already, and at the moment I see no one to look to, though Eden has made some good speeches. I met Professor Born* the other day, he looked stricken, and had just had news of friends in concentration camps and Micha Kohnstamm wrote me 'Practically every man we know has been arrested.'

"Janet du Cros† is at home, her husband comes over next month and is to have a year doing research with Born. They are staying at Regent Terrace with the two children, to keep Sir Herbert company. He is very depressed and melancholy and misses Lady Grierson terribly. I am delighted to have Janet in Edinburgh as you can imagine and see a good deal of them.

"What have you to tell me about Edward? – I have no child to tell you about of my own, but I must tell you about another I saw the other day, a fascinating creature with platinum hair, blue eyes, curiously set with very black lashes, age: 2 yr 7 months. I went for a walk with her and her mother, the child Stella in a pram. Every time I have seen her she has always been excessively tiresome and this was no exception. 'Mummy I want to get down and walk' she said 5000 times without drawing breath and I thought 'Heavens I could never be a mother.' At last after half an hour of conversation broken by this cry, we got on to the Pentlands Hills and the mother let the child down. In a moment she was flying on ahead in the teeth of a bitter wind and in an ecstasy of enjoyment such as I have never seen, hands in pockets, platinum locks flying, blue coat blown in the wind, chuckling, singing, calling to the birds that she could see in the fields through the hedgeroots – quite oblivious to us. We came to a burn and she stood saying 'Lovely water, lovely water.' It was one of the most entrancing things I've ever seen."§

---

* Max Born, the physicist
† Pianist, writer and broadcaster, fifth daughter of Sir Herbert Grierson and wife of François Teissier du Cros
§ Alison to Lyn from Edinburgh, 20 November 1938

ALISON'S first reaction to the prospect of another war with Germany was astonishment rather than horror. "How fantastic that this sort of thing should happen twice in our short life time." She regretted not being ten years younger to be in the thick of it and go freely into danger, and she welcomed the relaxation of social habits. Friends dropped in without ceremony; Max Born brought his huge Airedale ("Trixie – figure-toi!") and took her walking through the woods up to Craigmillar Castle. On the other hand – "How tiresome this living from week to week is. People are sick of talking of the international situation. I read myself to sleep every night on the Victorians. The best was *Middlemarch*, isn't it superb? Someone said to me once that no one under 30 should read it, which I feel is true. Had I read it younger I should simply have thought Dorothea a prig, but now that simplicity and generosity of character demands one's full assent. And the observation. Do you remember when Dorothea found Rosamund and Will together she went off riding on the tide of her anger to spend the evening in tremendous spirits at the vicarage until Will's name was mentioned in conversation, and everything went but wretchedness and she crept home to bite the carpet all night? No novel since *Le Rouge et le Noir* has so convinced me."*

That month I lived myself from day to day, waiting for the reluctant birth of my second child. "The envelope from you," wrote Alison on May 22, "the card from Max this morning. I had been flying daily to Births in the *Times* and thinking 'Not yet, poor Lyn.' I am so glad – not the girl you expected – 'Bring forth men children only.' But more fun for comparative purposes with Edward.

* Alison to Lyn from Edinburgh, 14 May 1939

78

"A morning from heaven, I can't tell you how beautiful. Chrysobel and Janet asked if they might go and see the Ld High Commissioner drive from Holyrood to St Giles before opening the Assembly. I said yes, and have just been seeing the parent into a taxi. Last night he said 'Would you mind looking at my gew-gaws to see if they have become fly-blown,' but went off pleased that he could get into his moderatorial dress of 15 years ago, though he muttered 'I shall go off in a plexy in the midst of St Giles.' My father sends you his love and congratulations. He says if the child is virtuous it will be happy."*

Realizing that it might be a long time before she could go abroad, more than half thinking the chance would never come again, Alison went to Geneva in June and picked up work there for a couple of months, renewing and strengthening her Genevan friendships. She returned to Edinburgh in August and Janet Teissier du Cros in her *Divided Loyalties*† describes the darkness and confusion of Waverley station on the night of September 1, as she and her husband – on the first step of their journey to France – were reduced to striking matches to find their compartment, and how Alison and two other friends broke through the barrier and ran down the platform to say good-bye.

Chrysobel who wished to see the Lord High Commissioner now appeared frequently in Alison's letters – "a most admirable girl from Strathdon. She comes from the best small-farming stock and has a good Aberdeen accent." On September 3 Alison and Chrysobel listened to Chamberlain's declaration together and exchanged a few grave remarks. Then Chrysobel said "Well, I think I'll away and give the dining-room a thorough." While the vacuum was humming Alison heard the air raid warning and went to tell Chrysobel. "We shut shutters and opened windows and then she said 'I'll maybe get the dining-room finished before they come.' Before the All Clear signal was given she emerged with a triumphant smile 'Weel we've got that over in spite of them anyhow.' My parent is well. He is finding solace or at least distraction in studying Federal Union and writing autobiographical memoirs. Now I must stop, a German lesson

* See *So much Love, So little Money*, p. 105, and p. 40 of this book
† Published by Hamish Hamilton in 1962

and then a four-hour shift in an A.R.P. post, a cold and stinking garage. I have just finished re-reading *Jane Eyre*, *Villette* and *Shirley*. A heavenly re-discovery."*

In the spirit with which she hoovered herself and Alison through the outbreak of war, Chrysobel saw the household at 13 Mayfield Terrace through the next six years; while the Cairns saw her through marriage and her first child. Alison travelled by taxi with her at midnight to the Simpson Maternity Pavilion, and she returned to Mayfield Terrace with the baby until her husband was demobilized. She was devoted to them all and would look D. S. Cairns over with the eye of a nanny when he was leaving the house, and deal with spots on the lapel of his coat or dust on the collar. She was devoted even to the cat, John, whose dislike for war-time scraps was to give much trouble. "He chaws it to right and he chaws it to left, makin' horrible grimaces. But gie him a bit o' fish, and it's over his throat wi' never the mark o' a tooth on't."

Immediately after Alison had sealed up her letter of October 16, the Germans visited Edinburgh. She heard the bombs and ran out of the house, and saw puffs of smoke in the sky, but no planes. At that moment her refugee arrived for the lesson in German. "He was in a very nervy state and to reassure him as well as myself I took the line that it was practise firing. We went on with our lesson. Loud pops were heard. 'What's that?' looking like a little startled hare. 'Traffic noises,' I said firmly. 'Very queer traffic,' said he, as indeed it was. As no sirens went, no one was alarmed, and when it was over, people were on the whole much exhilarated and pleased to think that Scotland had been the first place of attack. The sirens are horrifying. 'A note of doom' as my Chrysobel says in her good Aberdeenshire voice. What a tedious and terrible business it is. The parent is hopeful about the outcome but I take what he calls the 'apocalyptic view,' and from the completely selfish and personal point of view wish that it had come when I was ten years younger. Letters from French and Polish friends howl for the extermination of Germany – but no, revenons aux petits moutons, aux agneaux je dirais même. . . .

* Alison to Lyn from Edinburgh, 16 October 1939

"We visited the Borns the other evening. For the first time I saw the Jewish cast of his head and remembered what one of the Viennese refugees said to me here describing their life after the Anschluss. 'We couldn't talk about "cultural" subjects any more, only about who had got away and who had prospects of getting away, and one very strange thing was we all began to look more Jewish!' "*

D. S. Cairns was sustained not merely by the conviction that the God who had seen mankind through the Stone Age and the Iron Age, would not abandon his creation now, but also by specific opinions that should be remembered, since all prophetic vision is received with incredulity, but when fulfilled may be set aside as nothing more than human foresight. He had written to me in 1934 that Professor Piper, just then expelled from Germany, gave Hitler fifteen years, but to Cairns' mind that was too generous. Six years later when the power and prospects of Hitler had improved far beyond our worst fears, D. S. Cairns was still unshaken. 'We have all gravely under-estimated his power of Blitzkreig. I still gravely question his powers of endurance."

D. S. Cairns' serenity, Alison observed to Bess Tapper, was "something he has created for himself, for his natural man is extremely jumpy and apprehensive." She reminded Bess how apprehension had lifted its head not long before when Bess and Alison proposed going for a drive in the Trossachs with a friend whom Bess had acquired on the journey from Switzerland; whose credentials D. S. Cairns apparently thought insufficient. Since a wheel came off the car, his fears were partly justified. There were other small vulnerable points. "At a weekly inter-cession service held in the Usher Hall by all the churches, a Baptist, praying just before an address to be given by F. asked for a blessing on 'this thine aged servant.' F. opening his eyes saw 'Willie† heaving uneasily in his chair' with sympathy I suppose, and that evening as we sat reading in the study I heard an angry murmur 'Thine aged servant, indeed!' " In the same letter – "Did I tell you I had 'joined the church' as they say,

* Alison to Lyn from Edinburgh, 6 December 1939
† His brother

this last summer? Partly because our visit to Palestine last year did make me at last realise that the N.T. story was something that had actually taken place, partly because of last year's September crisis and the thought that the devil might win."*

At first Alison found work with the Edinburgh Refugee Committee, but that soon came to an end, and the promise to wardens of the first air raid also petered out. In the spring of 1940 she wrote to me "Even without a family and with two good maids one's days seem filled with le petit va-et-vient. It argues a dull spirit that it should be so and I often hope the subconscious is busy with something and will throw it up one of these days – I hope it won't be a monster. I have been reading Osbert Sitwell's novel *Those were the Days*, so depressing, as indeed it must have been to write – arid, successful intelligent people – there but for the g. of G. go A.H.C. and her friends – I used to smell that stale smell in the air in London. More convincing in the same lines was E. Bowen's *Death of the Heart* which I read about a year ago, books that made one feel it was about time for a war or some upheaval." As if to purify her thoughts she then gave me one of her beautiful pictures of Chrysobel. "She told me the other day that as it was spring she had decided she would like a new gas-mask case and added in matter of fact tones 'I got a very expensive one.' (So it was my dear, 7/6) 'But it was the one I liked best because its colour reminded me of a curlew's egg.' She went on to say that she had only heard one curlew since she came to Edinburgh. I asked her where and she said 'lying in my bed at night. It must have been flying over the house, they always cry when they're on the wing.' At home on the hill behind their farm they always knew if there were deer, or a fox, or a shepherd and his dog, or anything unusual on the hill for the curlews would set up such a crying." Yet after this she could add: "I think it must be one of the signs of growing middle-aged – the comparative difficulty with which one writes. I make myself sit down now when once I flew to pen and paper – what letters poured from our pens. Pages and pages on lined thin paper blocks the earliest ones were. I still have one or two

* Alison to Lyn from Edinburgh, 8 December 1938

of yours from this period. Some day when we are going to meet I shall collect them for you to read."*

Although we were indeed very fluent writers in our childhood, I cannot believe that those effusions were as easy to read as what came later, or that the trouble of finding words meant anything at all but increased sense and sensibility. I do regret that in this book so much that Alison left behind her must be omitted. When I return to the holographs to check a quotation or a date, I am dazzled by the richness of the pages that I felt obliged to pass over for reasons of space, or to preserve a fairly connected narrative. More scraps of gossip would make for liveliness, but she thought poorly of gossip for its own sake. Just before she left Aberdeen the wife of one of the professors took her aside to make a critical comment upon another wife, a woman known to both of us. "I don't know why I should be retailing gossip to you like this. One's mind plays about a situation and people, and it startles me when a cold gleam from the eye of a stranger falls upon an old friend."

When Alison went to Biggar for a short holiday in the summer of 1940, she found the town full of Poles, making a very good impression – "such beautiful manners." Her cousins the Pairmans whom she visited the first evening, had a Polish captain billeted on them – "extremely amusing, very charming," she wrote to Bess Tapper "I enclose his photograph. Do you recognize him?" This was Witold Langrod, an old friend of the Deutschman family, and of Bess too. "When we had mutually discovered the Deutschmans he asked me if I knew you. I said 'I had a letter from her this morning.' " In fact he had lived in Geneva from 1935 to 1939, working in the I.L.O. on the employment and migration of European population groups, and Bess had taught him his English. His friendship with Alison, planted firmly on this common ground could scarcely fail to thrive. This was one of the best windfalls of the war, to find in Biggar, that quiet little market town with all its sober ancestral connections, the home of people as calculable as my father† and the Pairmans, this

---

* Alison to Lyn from Edinburgh 27 March 1940

† I first wrote my father *and mother*, but reflected then that my mother was as incalculable as a wilderness of Witolds

incalculable Polish captain, an inspired *blagueur*. He did not stay there long, and the same wind that brought him down in Biggar continually caught him up and swept him along from one assignment to another in his war service. The Pairmans received a general in his place, but he did not replace Witold in their affections, and he remained as Alison noted "quite touchingly faithful" to these elderly people, and all his Scottish friends.

After two or three false starts, Alison found her place with the Ministry of Food. Early in 1942 she succeeded Muriel Watt as organizer of Food Advice for South-east Scotland. The centre of this department had been opened in an old shop near the foot of Leith Walk, with the office in a small dark room at the back; later on it moved to larger but scarcely healthier quarters in St Patrick Street near George Square. Alison's own ignorance of cooking turned out to be no handicap. She knew how to delegate work to her demonstrators, and her palate was always as sensitive as a child's. (I remember her eating a cream cracker, that most neutral of foods, hardly a food at all, near cousin to rice paper, and enjoying the flavour avidly, distinguishing on her palate the wheat flour, the salt, the water and the alchemy of the oven.) She travelled with her team all over the south-east area addressing meetings and showing what could be done to make the food available in wartime more nourishing and more interesting. The work gave Alison people, and places – which she loved only second to people – and finally it gave her a car. The wife of a miner in Fifeshire went straight to her heart by saying "Do you ever *read*, hen?" and then telling her the plot of the one book that she had read, a thriller in which the murderer made an omelet in the kitchen of his victim. Whatever Alison's hand found to do, she did it with all her might. I often observed her doggedness with admiration, and how she pushed back the threshold of boredom. It may be that she had an advantage over me by being a generation closer to the honest drudgery of farming life. She herself put it another way, saying "I'm not good at a job, because I get sunk in it," and Mary Trevelyan complained that Alison gave such whole-hearted attention to each vis-à-vis at Student Movement House, the rest for the time being might drown or hang as they wished. But now in

Food Advice she took great care of all her staff, inspecting their accommodation in out-of-the-way places, concerning herself in every particular with their health and happiness. Among the demonstrators she was particularly drawn to the youngest, Nancy Blackburn, a Lancastrian, like Alison's friend at Oriel College, Lady Ross.* Alone at the office one Boxing Day, Alison and Nancy talked about the freedom claimed by the new generation of young women, and Alison grew reminiscent and told Nancy the story of Belle-Ile and the Cremers and Francis and Graham, and the reaction of her father and her family to the adventures of 1921 – chiefly as a warning to Nancy not to let anyone stand between her and life. She told the story without indignation, but not entirely without bitterness.

Cigarettes were the toll that Alison paid for the pressure of life at the Food Advice Centre – *Passing Clouds* from the tobacconist over the way from the Centre, collected each morning as soon as the shop opened. The answer she had received from her specialist to the question "How long can I overdo it with impunity?" had been filed away for the duration. Significantly Witold Langrod approved a little black turban – costing nine and sevenpence, but transformed by an old paste shoe-buckle. "Oui, c'est très bien. Cela arrondit un peu le visage." They met occasionally in London when Alison was called up for meetings on Food Advice, and Witold's attachment restored the self-confidence she had lost in her early thirties. And now that Marthe Spender is freed from the self-regard which is a thorn in every living breast, I can quote without compunction from a letter that Alison wrote to David in 1944.† She was describing a recent visit to London.

"On Thursday Marthe Spender had invited Langrod and myself to lunch with her at a Czech Restaurant. This was vastly entertaining. Marthe is a great arranger, manager and promoter. I got to know Langrod so well because he was a friend of her

* When General de Gaulle stayed at Oriel during the war the two half-crowns which he left in his bedroom were pocketed by his incensed hostess. "Only you and Lady Ross could have done that," said Alison to Nancy; "you're both Lancastrians."

† Marthe Spender died in Paris in May 1966, to my grief and loss. I had visited her there in 1963 to talk of Alison, a meeting proposed as an hour over afternoon tea, which continued late into the evening over supper too.

sister's, and he also knew her. In a sense she felt she owned us both, and that so far as Langrod was concerned I was under her patronage. Langrod with his incredible quickness grasped this situation and played it up with sprightly malice, becoming demonstratively my very dear and intimate friend. I had lunch with him again 2 days later. He said 'Martha did not know we knew each other so well, no? I think she was a little cross, yes?' What a shame, but it was very funny. I am really very fond of M. with quite *warm* affection too, but she does so love to manage situations and set people right, one feels *justified* in asserting one's individuality by laughing at her. Incidentally Langrod has got her an excellent job in UNRAA, for which she is admirably fitted both by her considerable ability and her own experience as a P.O.W. I feel very pleased about it, both as a good thing happening to a friend, and also because all her efforts to keep her morale in camp – her study of languages, the part she played in organising the camp, the letters, almost solicitor's letters she wrote on behalf of Frenchwomen of British nationality in the camp – all this has made her an ideal person for the type of work she has been given to organise – virtue rewarded, a pattern in life."*

The regular Cairns family holidays which had counted for so much were now in abeyance. David was in the army, a chaplain with the Scots Guards, and they missed Jessie Cairns as hausfrau. Alison's leave was too short to warrant taking a cottage for herself and D. S. Cairns, even if she had felt equal to the labour of it, but she made two visits to Iona with Mary Trevelyan, and although it took twelve hours from Edinburgh to get there – and a military permit – a week on Iona, she reckoned, did her more good than a fortnight anywhere else. She and Mary, storm-stayed on Mull, went to the manse to ask for shelter, on a night as inclement as Lear endured, and were refused until Alison picked up a copy of her father's *The Riddle of the World* (the Baird Lectures over which she had worked so hard) and casually mentioned her relationship to the author. It was an incident which did nothing to lessen the riddle for Alison or Mary.

* Alison to David from Edinburgh, 1 November 1944

The Western Isles soon set their stamp on her subconscious, as a dream that she noted in her *Shriek Book* bears witness, a dream so neatly constructed that it demonstrates every facet of her life. She found herself on a rocky island like a cathedral with doors at either end. Willa Muir insisted on the doors being wide open to let sea and wind have free passage, which was awkward as it was in fact an orphanage under Alison's care. Crowds of little girl orphans lay in bed with the bed-clothes all awry, showing their nakedness, but Alison found that she did nothing at all about covering them up. "Father seemed to be there throughout though I was conscious of him rather than seeing or speaking to him, we were 'we.' There was a study on the island. A lady, it may have been Lydia Trout, said 'There aren't many good studies in Scotland.' I said 'I was in a manner of speaking brought up in a study and 3 or 4 studies and they were splendid studies.' Lydia and Nicolas seemed to indicate they wished they had *time* for study. I thought to myself, it is an essential. How can they with their not very powerful mental abilities think and gain anything from the amount or the quality of the kind of reading they do."

I T IS through Bess Tapper and Alison's letters to Bess that I know something of how she lived during the war, when I myself was far away and too busy to keep up a correspondence with anyone outside my own family. Marthe Spender, as the reader may have gathered, was a prisoner of war, interned in Vittel after the fall of France. Her three friends in Britain, Bess, Alison and Flora Burley, although widely separated, pooled resources and clothes coupons in order to send parcels to her. And this they continued faithfully until her release, although Marthe, owing to some inhibition, found herself unable to write a single word of thanks. Letters about her needs shuttled back and forth between Edinburgh, Aberdeen and Leicester, and Bess kept every line that Alison wrote to her, poring over the indecipherable words, thinking then and twenty years later "if only I could get it the whole world would be clearer." All Alison's friends can understand this. Once a letter that she wrote to me went astray, and I have never ceased to believe that if it could be found, no matter how late, I should live with more confidence and purpose after reading it. In fact Alison's letters to Bess at this time turn largely on the vexations caused by the absurd P.O.W. regulations (for example – pyjamas must be quite plain not striped), and on the many kindnesses of Bess to Alison herself. Occasionally she permitted herself the luxury of a *Shriek*.

"I am rather under the weather at the moment, and so have not much that is interesting or enlivening to say! Ah well we all have our battles and miseries, and that of the single woman approaching middle age is trivial enough compared to what the majority of people have to contend with. Still it feels like a fight too, as you dear Bess I daresay know also. What always cheers me as I gird my loins and pluck up my courage again is what Jacob said to the Angel that he wrestled with all night. 'I will not let thee go unless thou bless me.' It's an egotistical form of comfort, but one must take one's encouragements where one finds them."*

At the end of February 1944, Alison was summoned to a Food Advice Conference in Birmingham. Bess as a Labour Supply Inspector in Leicester was near enough to Birmingham for Alison to suggest that they should meet for the weekend after her conference. Bess picked Matlock and made the arrangements, and wrote in her notes eighteen years later: "Even to-day I can conjure up very easily the climate – physical and emotional – of that weekend. The hotel was luxurious by wartime standards; the country lay under thick snow; on our walks I remember each twig was outlined in white against the pale sun. We talked, we rested at stated times laid down by Alison's firm ruling. It was an enchantment from beginning to end." Bess had managed to bring a bottle of port and a home-made cake. For some obscure reason they listened in the lounge of the hotel to a radio pro-gramme for St David's day on Sunday 27 February. Alison as a Presbyterian had equivocal views on saints in general, but it was impossible to ignore one of that *name*. By the real St David's day both of them were back at work, but owing to the broadcast the weekend stood at March 1 in Alison's memory, and for many years she made a point of writing to Bess on that day, harking back to the pleasure that the holiday gave her – how looking into Bess's room on the Sunday afternoon, she had seen "the glow of the fire, you snug in bed, the snowflakes swirling past the window, the whole somehow seen through a luxurious glow of PORT."

It was one of those cherished times when the strength of her emotions seemed enough to overturn every obstacle to fulfilment. Neither she nor Bess had seen Witold for some time. He had turned up in Edinburgh the previous October, staying with "an ardent and jealous admirer, a Miss Robertson, aged 83." Alison had seen him off to the United States at Waverley Station – Witold in high spirits – and apart from a Christmas card, there had been no word since. Nevertheless she was confident of her importance to him. In the first hour at the Pairmans in Biggar

* Alison to Bess from Edinburgh, 5 April 1942

they had both experienced that mutual recognition which is something more than attraction, and so rare that it comes at most once in a life-time. Bess did not understand. She knew Witold well, knew him to be brilliant and amusing, and volatile. When she pointed out to Alison that he was married, even that scarcely seemed to discourage, for after all, Alison's intuitions had for years been steering her past the suitable match.

On Alison's long return journey by train to Edinburgh she hugged the impressions of the three days at Matlock and the long friendly talks with Bess, in which her heart had the comfort of being opened although it could never be satisfied. The exquisite taste of hope still alive had permeated every hour. As the dim and sightless train flogged its way through the night, I can imagine her repeating those words she had written after Brompton, *I must believe that some living principle will emerge.* And in fact before she left the train something happened – a trifle to anyone less agitated and sensitive, but to Alison at that time, a vision, helping her to move forward to take Witold on new terms. She found that the lavatory in her carriage was out of order, so she pushed across the gangway into the next carriage. It was unoccupied, and no one had turned on lights or pulled the blinds, and suddenly from the obscurity of the blackout she came face to face with unconceived beauty. The train was now passing through the Borders and snow had fallen heavily there too, but the moon was shining brightly on the country of her childhood and her ancestors, moors and hills rolling away so high and wide that she seemed to be on top of the world. Scales fell from her eyes as they fell from those of the young man who ministered to the prophet.

IT IS time to say something of Alison's connection with the group of people who came together in 1936, and, in an endeavour to preserve and foster Scottish traditions, had formed the Saltire Society. In the war Alison took charge of the Saltire publications – a heavy addition to her work and domestic responsibilities, but very congenial to her – and she was in consequence closely in touch with Robert Hurd, the architect, who became president of the society in 1943 for five years, and then honorary secretary until 1956. Robert was a man of exceptional parts, great taste, humour, humanity; charming and handsome into the bargain. He was not Alison's equal in quickness of mind and wit, but this was more from a strange timidity which sometimes gagged him (or made him cut an old friend in the street) than from bluntness of perception. He had never married, and did not choose to collect adoring women about him, and in their friendship Alison soft-pedalled her femininity, as she did with her father and David. But it was asking too much to expect her to be meek as well as unfeminine, and Robert's notorious, pathological unpunctuality and fits of farouche behaviour made her boil. FURIOUS, she would print in her diary, but the next day she was mollified by one of Robert's graceful notes of apology; or he came and talked and amused her. "I can forgive a man anything if he makes me laugh." When she had some game sent by her cousin Henry Aitchison at Lochton, she often asked Robert to lunch to enjoy the good fare, and herself was charmed when he returned hospitality by bringing her "2 pints of milk, a loaf of bread, half a pound of butter and some cooking fat."

How far Alison was from being meek and submissive in spirit came home to me in a curious way when we went together to see Greta Garbo in a revival of the film *La Dame aux Camélias*.

We had both seen it a quarter of a century earlier, I to be fascinated but Alison then to jeer. At this revival she found it better
than she remembered, though not as compelling as I did. "L. in
tears, me not," she wrote in her diary. For me there was no
quarter of a century. We discussed it with much interest afterwards. The well-known scene in which Marguerite to prevent
discovery, drowns the sound of Armand's frantic ringing at the
door by her arpeggios and laughter, had set my heart racing
with shame and alarm, but Alison felt nothing but indignation
on behalf of de Varville, the deceived protector.

The partnership between Robert and Alison was extremely
fruitful for the Saltire Society, and Robert gave Alison new
friends, notably – in 1944 – Agnes Mure Mackenzie the Scottish
historian whom Alison grew to admire deeply, describing her as
"a passionate, prejudiced creature with a witty incisive mind,
and great elegance of person, a woman of style and warmth of
heart." After their first meeting Agnes wrote to Robert "I had
less talk with A.C. than I would have liked, as her father
plunged me up to the neck in Flodden. A friend of his has a
theory which whitewashes the Earl of Home and as a Border
man he hopes it is true. A. is one of the people I shall hope to
know better if we come north. We seem to talk the same
language, and I think we could be friends."*

In a superficial sense they did not talk the same language at
all, for Agnes's was faintly tinged with whimsicality. Alison's
infrequent use of Scots was always dry and valuable – "*who all
were there?*" – "*the caller wind*" – and she must have winced
very slightly to see Agnes describe the Saltire Chapbooks† as
"bonny bit bookies." But they became friends at once over the
publication by Oliver and Boyd for the Saltire Society of Agnes's
first *Scottish Pageant*, in her series of successful anthologies.
Agnes had barely finished quarrelling with Oliver and Boyd over
another work, so Alison's first task was one of reconciliation. She
kept all the letters from Agnes and carbon copies of her own
replies through 1944 and 1945, and they were soon "Agnes" and
"Alison" and advising one another about clothes and cats and

* Agnes and her sister Jean were still living in London at this time
† One of Alison's most brilliant publishing ideas

frozen cisterns. Presently Alison put forward two of her favourite ideas, working in her characteristic way, finding the right soil and conditions, and as soon as the ideas had taken root, passing on, quite indifferent as to who (*who all*) might get the credit. She consulted Agnes about a new Statistical Account of Scotland, a century having passed since the second one appeared. Agnes saw the value of the suggestion, but the work involved in this task alarmed her. "An all-Scotland one would take a mighty lot of editing and of money for printing. I wonder if it would be possible to have simply typed copies available in the Saltire headquarters of the big cities and free for consultation." Where Alison next peddled this idea, I do not know, but she worked fast and well for in 1946 the Registrar-General for Scotland, Mr J. G. Kyd, publicly stated "what many were feeling," that the time was ripe for a Third Statistical Account, and with the help of the Nuffield Trust the Scottish Universities undertook the task. The first handsome volume (Ayrshire) appeared in 1951, published by Oliver and Boyd.

In January 1945, Alison writing to Agnes about her *Scottish Pageant* asked if she could not include at least part of the Arbroath Declaration – the letter written in 1320 by the Lay Estates to Pope John XXII asking for his support in their endeavour to secure Scottish independence and an honourable peace with Edward II. "It is surprisingly little known, and really very inaccessible to the ordinary reader. I know the S.N.P. published it in a leaflet, but how many people see that?" Agnes was unenthusiastic. She thought she had worked "the really juicy bits" into her editorial comment. "The whole declaration is rather long, and much of it is an historical summary, not very lively." Alison let the matter drop for three months, and then returned to her point with increased vigour. "People just don't know about it. Ian Finlay never mentioned it in his new little book. I only knew about it myself a few years ago when my father à propos of something turned it up as something he had forgotten about, and I was brought up in a very strong Scottish tradition. I've shown it to lots of people since – university lecturers and so on, who had never heard of it. I'm carried away every time I read it. It's the very genius of our people that speaks in the Declaration, and I've heard it at student meetings and in argument and yes, even in the General Assembly."

"I honestly thought," replied Agnes, "that even our country knew about Arbroath. In any other it would be in all the schools. We teach them about Magna Carta and don't at that inform them it was largely secured by a king of Scots. After what you say it had better go in. I must make a new translation, though. Never seen a good one. They all lack punch and ring." A few days later the translation followed. "Alison my dear, you were quite right. I beat my head on the mat, though I do not chew it. Here is a full translation – the only one I ever ever seen. I have done my best to keep it as close as possible, but to get the drive and ring of the Latin – which has that."

It was this translation which became the authorized version of the Arbroath Declaration and was used in the first Arbroath Pageant and has been frequently used since.*

I have not finished yet with 1944. It was the year that Alison's uncle Willie Cairns died after a short illness. Alison wrote to Bess describing the dignity and confidence with which he had approached death, like his brother John and his sister Jessie. "It's curiously reassuring," said Alison, "to one of our rather battered and uncertain generation." She had a new anxiety to meet that summer. On the invasion of France David went abroad with his regiment, and it was less easy to welcome danger for him than for herself. Nancy Blackburn at Food Advice was conscious of the fearful strain under which Alison lived from June 1944 until VE Day, and realized from the references to her brother that this was the relationship which overtopped all others in her life; as I am sure it was.

The retreat of the German army brought the liberation of the prisoners in Vittel and Marthe Spender came to Edinburgh to stay with the Cairns for a month. D. S. Cairns talked to her

* The Arbroath Pageant owed its existence largely to Margaret Brodie, at one time editor of the *Arbroath Herald*, and her successor on the paper, George Shepherd, and also to F. W. A. Thornton. A celebration of the sexcentenary of the Declaration which took place in 1920, had degenerated "into a very unworthy kind of all-dancing, all-singing, folksy jamboree," (I quote Mr Shepherd) unlike the later revivals under distinguished sponsors, with Agnes Mure Mackenzie as one of the vice-presidents.

of Alison's future, and his deep regret that she had not married. He knew, he said, "when it came to the point" she would never agree to marry anyone, and he was to blame, at least in part, for having expected so much from her. But Alison had been distracted from marriage as much by the claims her father satisfied as by those he made. He had been too lively and profitable a companion; and unexpectedly malleable as the years went on. Alison had kept him young, influenced his views, taught him to tolerate her offering sherry to their visitors, and flung heresies at him across the dinner table as they discussed the Sunday sermon. She applied her lipstick in his presence while he groaned – "If you could see yourself with that bloody gash designed to *mash* young men." When Alison went down to the Caley to see him off to Iona in 1944 – he was then eighty-one – they had an argument on the platform "in the course of which I was obliged to call him an obstinate old gannet. Do not be pained, it was all v. good-tempered, but that pig-headed old man wanted on the return journey to travel from Iona, arrive in Edinburgh abt. 4.45, and then take a bus (w. ages standing in a queue) to go out to Broughton." The following November after he had been three days indoors with a bad cold, he insisted on going out to dine with some cronies on the other side of the town, although the night was "windy, rainy, and black as pitch, no taxis to be had." He returned in high good humour, "remarking à propos of the wind that he had not felt so insecure on his feet for 70 years. The reference was to the night of the Tay Bridge disaster!" She had scribbled down on a piece of paper her mixing him up with God as a child, and then how she had seen him with the eyes of maturity when he was preaching in King's College Chapel, Aberdeen, "... in black preaching gown, moderator's, very neatly gathered at the shoulders on the back. F. looks very fine very dignified, quite unselfconscious, serious, devout, much the most picturesque and w. the finest head in King's College Chapel." She did not exaggerate, and his expression in old age was wonderfully shrewd as well as candid; there was a combination of peasant wit and holy wisdom shining there. One of God's spies, he was, who had taken upon himself the mystery of things.

95

D. S. Cairns was not alone in his concern about Alison's future. Returning from a meeting at Jedburgh, Alison met her old governess, the dragon of her childhood, coming down the path from 13 Mayfield Terrace. "She would not return to the house with me but stayed talking in a rather high voice and on a very high note which I was convinced must be overheard by the Steins, advised me to get married as otherwise I would have a very lonely old age. I said all very well but even then I might be left a widow but she replied that at least that wd. not be my own choice. Poor C.M. – on reflection I was very much touched at her concern. She is remarkably brisk for 80, eye bright, blue-grey, hair still gingery, step very light and quick – in every way recognisable but very small and twitchy poor old thing. We seem to have been very much a feature in her life, as indeed she was in ours, but one cannot feel rancour at anyone so small and old."*

Early in 1946 D. S. Cairns fell ill, and an operation for cancer became suddenly necessary, but he rode this wave very calmly, quite prepared for death and satisfied that he had finished the work that he had been given to do. He appeared for some months to be making a good recovery, but in June the action of his heart began to fail. In the second week of July he became bed-ridden, and died on the 27th of that month. Alison and David had nursed him, "So we were very much together," she wrote to Bess. "It was a strange and moving experience and one that I am deeply glad to have gone through. You will know what I mean when I say that in a sense one feels bereft, yet in another sense it is not so, for that quality of character does seem to transcend mortality."

A few days after the death of D. S. Cairns I came to Scotland to visit my parents at Biggar. On Bank Holiday, August 5, about nine in the evening, there was a ring at the door and there stood Alison and David. It was the first time that Alison and I had met since 1938, and we found a great deal to say. We did not immediately speak of their bereavement. As the time passed – it was short enough for they were driving back to Edinburgh – it became clear that no one would grasp the lever and switch the

* Alison to David from Edinburgh, 8 September 1944

points. After they had gone my father and mother and I sat quite abject that it could have been so, very well aware that the man whom we had not mentioned would never himself have failed in such a situation. Alison put it right in a letter to my father, written on August 9.

"It was strange that we were so carried away by the pleasure of seeing you all again after so long the other evening, that we did not speak of what is always in our minds just now. I have to thank you for the very kind letter you sent us immediately after my father died. I told Lyn on the telephone, and she I am sure would tell you, how my father's strength began to fail at the end of June. . . . He was in bed for only a fortnight before he died, and suffered only during the last days, from great weakness. But until the last day or so when he became unconscious he was completely himself. We had much talk together and often he would make David and me laugh with one of his characteristic remarks. Late one afternoon – he had been very weak in the morning – he revived considerably and sat propped up by pillows, smoking a cigarette. I said something about his rubber air-ring cushion, which he hated, and he exclaimed with great vehemence 'That saddle is most unsuitable for the transit from time to eternity.' David and I shouted with laughter and he sat wreathed in smoke with a veiled look of amusement, rather pleased I think with the success of his comment.

"For months I had been dreading the funeral service, so unnecessarily as it turned out. It was all he would have wished – the sunshine, the flowers, the great number of friends, the deep sense of affection and gratitude in the service for the long rich full life completed.

"I have written rather at length for I know how fond you were of my father and he of you and Mrs Irvine. I remember those regular Saturday afternoon walks you and he used to have in the far-back days in Aberdeen.

"We did enjoy our visit to you on Monday, it was lovely to be with such old and dear friends."*

My father was three years younger than D. S. Cairns, and three years later he followed him. I had gone to Biggar for the

* Alison to the Rev. John A. Irvine, 9 August 1946

last weekend of June. On the Saturday evening my father and I stood in the garden by his study window admiring a yellow rose that had bloomed that day and was now filling the air with its scent, when we heard through the window my mother singing a verse of Watt's *There is a land of pure delight* in a soft yet clear and true voice.

> Could we but climb where Moses stood,
>   And view the landscape o'er;
> Not Jordan's stream, nor death's cold flood,
>   Should fright us from the shore.

We looked quickly at one another, touched and awed, and my father murmured in astonishment "She's *singing!*" On the Sunday he went off (in good time as his custom was) to take the morning service at the old parish church of St Mary's, since the minister was on holiday. He walked by the back road which gave more shade – the weather was exceedingly bright and warm – and I followed a little later by the main street, and after saying my prayer, sat in the cool and still church with my eyes on the pulpit, waiting for the beloved and now venerable head to appear. But when the minister entered the pulpit it was not my father. Such metamorphoses do happen in dreams and then we accept them, but in actual life credulity is painfully jolted. The strange face looked at us gravely and the strange voice informed us that my father was dead. Later in the day when my mother and I took comfort in the circumstances of his death for his sake, I mentioned her singing the evening before and the wonder that she should have chosen just that hymn and just that verse. She looked at me in amazement and assured me that she had never sung it, in fact her singing voice had entirely left her some years before. I wrote to tell Alison of this and all that had happened, knowing how easily she would enter into the strange atmosphere of those few days. "What can one wish better," she replied, "for one's old people or for oneself when the time comes, than such a death. Lyn do you know what my most vivid recollection of him is – it's a very early one for it goes back to Hamilton Place, indeed I'm not sure that it wasn't Rubislaw Terrace, for he and I were sitting in the big sunny bow-window, he in an ecstasy of enjoyment over a George Morrow joke in *Punch* – a very sickly looking Cleopatra having her pulse felt by an early Egyptian doctor 'Hm . . . Have we been drinking pearls again?' I think that must have been the first grown-up joke I ever 'saw,' and it came over mostly through your father's intense pleasure."*

---

* Alison to Lyn from Montana July 1949. The Morrow cartoon in the series "Marginal Notes on History" had appeared in *Punch* 28 February 1912, when Alison was nine.

THE DEATH of D. S. Cairns had nothing but well and fair about it. He knew that his work was completed and he departed without distress. Neither Alison nor David could feel really bereft, as she said. Yet after a few weeks Alison found herself in need of reassurance and went down to the old house called Nunlands, near Foulden – run at that time as a guest house – as if reassurance must come from the soil itself. By the river which her father described as his heart's anchorage and in the fields so familiar to them both, she found courage to begin an entirely different life. Almost all her forty-four years had been spent in the company of her father, always in vivid communication, even if it were to protest and lose her temper, and aware of the nobility of his nature even when she felt most critical. In her youth it had been a struggle to put him first; then a time came when this was so habitual that she found it difficult to do justice to herself. The father-daughter, mother-son kinships are notoriously pathogenic, but eventually between D. S. Cairns and Alison a relationship was established in which "we were we" and yet both were free in essentials, and it would be hard to say which of them gained more. The wisdom of age never grew stagnant with D. S. Cairns; Alison kept it in healthy and vigorous movement.

There were still the two Highland aunts at Granby Road, and her aunt Barbara and uncle Jo Aitchison, after handing over Lochton to their son Henry and his wife, had come to live in Frogston Road West. Through them some of the old ties with the Borders were maintained, and Harry Niel's meeting with the devil at Foul Fords was kept in mind.* It was Aunt Barbara who

* This interesting story, told by Andrew Lang on p. 269 of his *Dreams and Ghosts* (Longmans 1897) had been told to Barbara Craw when she was about twelve by her father's shepherd at Rawburn, John McLeish, and he had been one of the men who found the body of Niel's son, the devil's hostage. McLeish had seen the semmit (vest) on the dead man pulled over his other clothes, a common practice to ward off evil spirits.

at eighty thought of the wheel of her car as a very poor substitute for reins, and never saw a horse without craving to spring in the saddle. Beyond this inner circle, now so shrunken, ranged all the younger relatives and connections who helped to make Edinburgh the one city where Alison felt entirely at home.

"I saw Jean Ritchie the other day. I was passing a little shop in S. Clark St called WATT'S DOLLS' HOSPITAL and saw her standing in front of the window *transfixed* in front of a large white card displayed therein which was headed DOLLS AND ANIMALS EYES. Underneath in every size and colour were pairs of eyes connected with wire and marked Clear Rabbit, Pink Rabbit, Panda, Golliwog, Googoo and Sleeping Baby. She wheeled round when I tapped her on the shoulder and we burst out laughing. As we talked I began to notice how like Henry Aitchison she was – something in the angle of the face, and then the eyes and the bridge of the nose, uncannily like Uncle James. I said 'Heavens Jean how frightfully Craw you are.' "*

From this time on Alison kept a diary very regularly. It replaced, although inadequately, the chat over the day's doings late at night in her father's study. She went about a great deal and wrote down the names of the friends whom she met in the evenings after work, squeezing "Exhausted" into the last corner of the crowded segment on the blue pages of the slim leather-bound pocket book. Writing so tiny and difficult could scarcely be intended for even her own reading, but as life tumbled past like a burn in spate, these notes established her lien on it. She was acquiring a better and better grasp of contemporary Scotland, the kind of knowledge which in former days lifted government among the arts. It was becoming rare for her to meet anyone in all respects strange – without some ancestor or relative, some homestead or interest known to her, and the speed with which she discovered the tie that made the new acquaintance part of her life was not quite human. Nor was this skill limited to people. When I found a coloured print of Hawick in a back-street shop in Carlisle and sent it for her birthday, she wrote:

"How clever of you to find that enchanting little print of Hawick which I am delighted to have. This is Hawick as

* Alison to David from Edinburgh, 8 September 1944

William and Dorothy Wordsworth must have seen it, and as described in the autobiography of Rev. Mr Somerville minister of Jedburgh who explained to Charles James Fox who the Seceders were exactly, and after whose daughter-in-law Somerville College, Oxford took its name."

To her relief, she was not obliged to leave Mayfield Terrace at once. Besides all her own and her parents' books and papers it stored many of the contents of 20 Braidburn Crescent, and *that* house had taken over all the family treasures from 10 Spence Street. The ponderability of the accumulated possessions and relics of the generations whose lives had been devoted to the imponderable was truly astonishing. They ought by rights to have produced large families to absorb or destroy it, but the interests and habits that created the problem had helped to turn them from marriage (or at least made celibacy tolerable) and bound them one to another in the bundle of life. So the eight children from Dunglass had produced only four, and those four only two. Alison and David constituted the only young of a once prolific family and the whole burden of inheritance fell upon them.

Longing for a change of work, Alison applied for the position of secretary to the Royal Geographical Society, but without success. The Saltire Society was considering the appointment of a part-time secretary, but at a salary much less than she received in the Ministry of Food, and the money left by her father had not made her independent. To Bess she wrote:

"I have a feeling that changes are imminent though I do not see them clearly as yet. My two old aunts are very frail and I do not think I can leave Edinburgh while they are still alive – but anyhow I don't really want to, though I do want a change of job and a change of circumstances. I have been overworked lately and am suffering from fatigue, and what is more intolerable, that kind of mental and spiritual atrophy that overtakes me when overtired. Next week however I hope to cut away to my cousins in Berwickshire and recover. The very stamps on your last letter – the cyclamen and the primula gave me most exquisite pleasure."* For Bess had returned to Geneva after the

* Alison to Bess from Edinburgh, 17 May 1948

war. "Ah Génève!" cried Alison when she first heard this. "One cannot be lost or depressed there as in London – I always feel *there* that the whole vast city weighs upon me, there's something barbaric about it."

One of the predicted changes came soon after this with the engagement of David to Rosemary Russell – "a charming ½ Scots ¼ Irish girl whom he met in Oxford. Her father is a Science don at Christchurch – she's a good deal younger than David – about 27. I find it very rejuvenating." Rosemary turned out to be a sister after Alison's heart, cultivated, pretty and elegant, with more Irish than Scot in her. David had been elected to the chair of Practical Theology at Aberdeen and now bought a house there – in Hamilton Place in fact – and the wedding was fixed for December 1948.

That summer we were on family holiday at Borth-y-Gest in North Wales and persuaded Alison to join us for ten days. A water-colour sketch of her sitting in our little Welsh parlour reminds me how youthful she still looked with her dark glossy hair and her debonair carriage. But the fatigue that she had mentioned to Bess was still with her and she deplored being so out of condition that the first steep five hundred feet of Carn Goch winded her completely. She returned from this inadequate break to the fearsome task of going through all the family papers in the basement of Mayfield Terrace in preparation for giving up the house that winter. September was a bad month and the basement damp, and heaven knows what may still have been alive there among the books and papers and the dust. Alison caught one of her influenza colds and retired to bed, and afterwards took a few days at Cambus O' May to recuperate. When she returned, her lungs were X-rayed, but the pictures showed everything in good order. Yet in a very short time she was down with more influenza. Even in bed she went through family letters, and as soon as she was up she started typing out copies of Sir Herbert Grierson's letters to her father for inclusion in his autobiography, which she and David were now preparing for publication. At the end of November she visited a chest specialist and the earlier verdict about her lungs was revoked. On December 2 she wrote to David:

"This is just to thank you for your most comforting, most encouraging letter. It has cheered me a lot, and my dear creature I fear you must have gone out late to send it expressed, or did you take it to the station this morning? It arrived before lunch. Thank you for all the kind things you say – of course my dear D I should say they are not true, but I don't pause to ask myself if they are true. I simply purr. O yes indeed I have thought of the parent and the old 'uns. What a queer experience this is – part of it is screwing up one's own courage and part of it just handing it over and saying 'I've got to leave it to You' – rather an ungracious way of asking for help but there it is. But it's so contradictory – the active and the passive I mean."

It was impossible for her to go to David's wedding, a bitter disappointment, but in a very short time her wonderful spirits had revived. "I must say it is heavenly to look forward to some months of leisure. I feel I have been delivered from the machine. I lie snug amongst my pillows admiring my bulbs, now flowering, reading as I please, receiving visits, looked after by my kind Isobel." I had sent her two books from my own recent reading – Alain Fournier's *Le Grand Meaulnes* and Cyril Connolly's *The Unquiet Grave*. The resemblance between Fournier's romance and her holiday on Belle-Ile did not occur directly to her, but she was fascinated. "It has that absolutely compelling quality that stories used to have in one's youth. 'What can happen next?' And the atmosphere is living – that schoolroom in winter – the winter Sundays – the fête in the mansion. The Connolly amused me a bit at the time, but I don't think I can remember a single observation or reflection that he made. He's so tired and he made me tired too, but I was interested to see it as completing my impression of him."*

Midhurst had a long waiting list, but on February 6 Alison heard that Montana Hall in Switzerland could give her a room in two weeks' time. She arranged to fly with a nurse-escort from Prestwick to Geneva and wrote to Bess who booked rooms at the Hotel Cornavin. Bess suggested bringing a friend to visit her, but Alison answered cautiously. "I should like to see your friend too – but I do get tired very easily and shall have been

* Alison to Lyn from Edinburgh, January 1949

travelling since 8 that morning – I don't quite like to suggest that he or she should come as I might not feel up to seeing her or him!" Bess accordingly arrived alone, but after she had talked for a little, Witold walked into the room and regardless of Bess and the nurse and the bacilli, embraced Alison fondly.

Very soon from Montana Hall she wrote assuring David and Rosemary and all her friends that she felt very well indeed. Para-aminosalicylate had brought down her temperature and reduced her cough to almost nothing. Her windows and balcony in the sanatorium looked across the Rhone Valley to the Rothorn, Weisshorn, Gabelhorn and Matterhorn. "I do feel that some of my hardworked friends could well do with a little of the agreeable relaxation and leisure I am having." It came as a complete surprise when Dr Roche told her that she had been far too ill on her arrival to stand any operation. "Who would have thought it?" she wrote to David.

"I had my fortnightly examination with Roche y'day. I like him. He showed me my tomograms on a lit screen showing a cavity the size of an egg. 'Now that's a *beautiful* picture,' said he, pointing to one. 'More beautiful to you than to me,' said I. His wife died a year ago and he married the matron of this place. She is very pretty and has beautiful embroidered strings to her cap. After I had been here a week she came to see me and chatted away. I hadn't the faintest idea who she was and at last said in my most accomplished society tones 'I don't think we have met before, have we?' 'I'm Mrs Roche,' said she, but I kept my head and very graciously extended the right hand saying 'O *how* do you do.' "*

While she was at Montana an appreciation of D. S. Cairns by Donald Baillie was broadcast by the B.B.C. on the Home Service, and David sent Alison the script. "I think it's very good, but I don't think the parent quite comes through – none of the humour for instance or that kind of genial charm with which he met people without sacrificing any of his own integrity in the desire to please. Well you can't get everything into a 15 minute broadcast and such as it is, it is well done. But you couldn't imagine the subject of it exclaiming 'Unmoor yon

* Alison to David from Montana, 29 March 1949

skiff,'* could you, or developing that crazy game in which each stage of dressing was timed and had a particular name (I think putting on the shirt was termed Warroosh) in order to overcome the tedium of getting into one's clothes. I have been trying to remember how much of it comes out in the parent's own autobiographical material. It certainly was one of the qualities that people *enjoyed* most about the parent. When they tell stories of him or quote remarks that he made they are often in illustration of just that."†

Dr Roche decided that as soon as Alison was fit she must return to Midhurst for the permanent collapse of one-third of the right lung. There could be no resumption of normal life before the spring of 1950 at the earliest. She flew back to England in July but two months passed before her first operation and another two before she was writing letters again.

"Well I am all right, but everything has taken longer and been more complicated than expected. My old lung was too tough and resistant, like a leather football, to go down in two operations, so I had to have three, ordinarily there should have been a fortnight between each, but just before the third I got a superficial infection in the healed wound of the other two – this made me feel much more ill than all the surgery – but it was finally got the better of by penicillin. Now the doctors are v. pleased with me though I still have a certain amount of pain and discomfort. They say I shall only lose the use of $\frac{1}{4}$ to $\frac{1}{3}$ of one lung and apparently one hardly ever uses that anyway. I shan't begin to get up till abt. Jan and will be here till March or April."§

Although Alison was still a civil servant, on sick leave from the Ministry of Food, Food Advice had closed down in 1948, and as a wartime recruit, her salary was reduced with this change. She did not know what kind of post would be offered her when she was discharged fit nor even if it would be in Edinburgh. "I *hate* the *State*," she wrote to Nancy Blackburn but she had to live, and to live she had to earn. She was invited to apply for

* Meaning "Kindly pass the jam"
† Alison to David from Montana, 11 May 1949
§ Alison to Bess from Midhurst, 23 November 1949

the post of warden at a university hostel for women in Edinburgh and did so with alacrity, but her medical history discouraged the committee. She accepted this new disappointment without bitterness. "I see their point of course, but it's tiresome, for my doctors here say that I am a much safer subject now than at any time since 1935, and while most ex-T.B. patients are not taken back into the fighting forces, men who like me have had a thoracoplasty are readmitted even as pilots. Ah well, who knows what will emerge. I have an idea you know Bess, that I was getting very middle-aged and addicted to my comforts in Edinburgh and that being pitched out into the world like this may not be insalutary. I do want to go back to Edin. to live and work there if I can, but life will certainly be a more precarious less comfortable affair, and tant mieux perhaps. What an egotistic outpouring."*

In spite of her ability and her capacity for hard work, Alison's ostensible career was desultory and full of disappointments. The record of all she had done since leaving Girton was too various to be meaningful. But there was her other life, in which, unencumbered by holy orders, and as it were cloaked with invisibility through being a woman, she followed the long pastoral tradition of her ancestors, the Browns, the Cairns and the Smiths, feeding the lambs of God.

The summer of her release from hospital her father's auto-biography came out, very quietly for a book so remarkably humorous and original – and by a man widely known. But in the book world the channels of communication were already becoming blocked by the feverish over-production of publishing firms. Critics were jaded and booksellers had grown sour. "My dear D, I went into each of the Princes St Booksellers y'day and saw no copies lying anywhere. On Monday Stewart and Paula and Henry and Margaret† all came to shop and to tea. Henry and Stewart were perfectly sweet – thanking us warmly and enthusiastically – they had got their copies on Sat. and had been dipping in, kept saying which bits they had liked, and 'That was a good story' and 'I could just hear uncle David

* Alison to Bess from Midhurst, 11 April 1950
† The Aitchison cousins and their wives

saying this' (Stewart) and so on. It was very heartwarming and nice." She had shortly returned from a holiday with David and Rosemary. "My dear D I can't tell you how much good my six weeks with you have done. You and Ro have been most awfully good to me. I think of you both constantly and wish I could give you back some of the encouragement and confidence you have given me."*

When she came to stay with us at Cross Farm she looked well, but she still had a cough, rather worse than two years earlier. Surgery had brought about a sensitive and relaxed condition in the bronchial tubes, so that any change in the atmosphere made her cough, and – most cruel – laughing often triggered off a paroxysm. She hardly ever mentioned this affliction and if I looked my concern, she responded with a slight smile, but a shadow used to pass across her eyes, normally so brilliant and clear.

Her attitude to the weather now changed entirely, and she no longer felt the satisfaction carried right through from childhood, of pitting her strength against wind and frost and snow. The Edinburgh winter became her most formidable enemy, and January "quite my least favourite month." In fact it was not at first advisable to face this test and she spent the winter of 1950–51 and part of the following winter at Street with Roger and Sarah Clark putting the Clark family papers in order. She found the material "fascinating – like one of those novels about three generations of a big industrial family, that were so popular 10 or 15 years ago – only this is more interesting than any novel, for the characters create themselves in one's consciousness, and I am living in and with the family which is still of the same fabric."† Whitenights, the Clarks' house, was a mile from the village of Street and three from Glastonbury, "where Joseph of Arimathea brought the Holy Grail, where Arthur and Guinevere are buried, a most ancient holy place with I think still a slightly uncanny atmosphere." She lived quietly in great sympathy with her elderly host and hostess and enjoyed the Somerset spring, the

---

* Alison to David from Edinburgh, 26 September 1950

† See p. 56. "Roger," Alison wrote to Bess, "is a grandson of John Bright who was largely instrumental in getting the Corn Laws repealled. They were all Quakers, great Liberals, many in Parliament, the women great suffragists and feminists, all very philanthropic."

violets and aconites and snowdrops of which we had been robbed thirty years earlier by D. S. Cairns' fears for our virginity.

Alison had refused an invitation to spend the winter of 1950–51 with cousins in South Africa because of the age and frailty of the two aunts in Edinburgh, but when both were taken ill and died within a very short time of one another, the doctor at Street refused to let her travel north. To David she wrote on March 7:

"It sounds as if it had been a *very good funeral* and to have had a fine day and a great crowd of friends is a great comfort. I remember how those two factors were somehow so cheering on the day of the parent's funeral. Well there really is nothing to mourn except that 'Time like an ever-rolling stream bears all its sons away.' I remember once in my little bedroom at 62 Hamilton Place, suddenly waking up in the middle of the night with an appallingly vivid consciousness of this, and oddly enough it was the thought of Aunt K. and Uncle Willie and Aunt Elspeth and all their richness of memory and their youth in the far north being swept away on that flood, that cut me to the very heart. In one way I felt it more poignantly than I do now for it was one of those experiences that had the keen quality of a revelation. My one *great* regret is that neither you nor I were there that last day, but Eva Martin, an older connection than either of us, mercifully was. I shall miss them both frightfully, though they were in a way a care and a responsibility, they were still one's elders and bestowed so much affection and interest on us, in a way that no one else really can, and they were so independent and never made any claims. I used to go down and see them practically every week after we went to Mayfield Terrace and specially since Uncle Willie's death and they always gave me such a welcome and were such good company. All the time I was growing up and in rebellion, I counted on Aunt K. really more than on any of our relations by blood for sympathy and good advice. I have often thought what an enrichment it was to our whole family circle when Uncle Willie persuaded Aunt K. to marry him – the personal [? word omitted] of course, and over and above, that knowledge and feeling for the Highlands and a different tradition to our own. They brought us nothing but good those three bless them.

"Think my dear of deciding what is to be done with the spinning wheel and the African idol that used to stand in the study at Howard Place, and all the water-colours of Tongue and Caithness! It's not just a question of sweeping everything into store as at 13 Mayfield Terrace – it's more like the breaking up of Braidburn Crescent which was done by the Parent, Aunt K., Uncle Willie and me. Mercifully there is nothing like the mass of papers."*

No, but every cupboard and chest of drawers and wardrobe at Granby Road was stuffed to bursting point with clothes. Some were old and stylish enough to be acceptable at the Gateway Theatre, and there were some fine shawls and plaids, but the rest – what to do with the rest? Alison shot them off in all directions "to Ministers' widows, Personal Friends, City Cleaning Dept., Salvation Army, Eventide Homes," accepting this duty like the loving niece that she had been, not resenting it as much as some women might. I never observed her rebel at the trouble of feminine affairs. Merely to avoid being odd or slatternly a woman is involved in a multiplicity of decisions and routines unknown to men; while to achieve style, as Alison latterly did, takes time and thought and money. She took charge submissively of the paraphernalia of a dressy woman, always picked *Vogue* out of the magazines on a station bookstall – investigated scents – bought costume jewelry – and at one time had accumulated twenty-six hats, of which she jettisoned fourteen in one of her splendid clearings. She wrote after one of these "in a beautiful frame of mind, purged, absolved, starting life anew." A superficial litter in her bedroom witnessed to the upheaval, "but fundamentally I am clean and ordered, I can start life from my own roots again, life will become simple from to-day." This was a joke. She knew that it could never become simple, but this was how Alison – born "one of Nature's sluts" – reconciled herself to the drudgery of daily existence. She had been much impressed to learn from David that it had lifted his depression in the squalor of the war in Europe to take meticulous care – as far as the campaign permitted– of his own equipment and possessions.

Now with the departure of the Highland aunts, almost all the

* Alison to David from Street, 7 March 1951

guests of honour at the party had said farewell, only Aunt Barbara and Uncle Jo Aitchison still remained. On the sixth anniversary of her father's death, Alison wrote to David:

"To-day I was at church and drove past 20 B.B.C. and 13 Mayfield Terrace, mentally dipping my flag as it were in salute, for it is thirteen years since dear Aunt Jaye died and six since the Parent left us. Strange to think of them and the Willies and all that richness of life having passed from this world – having slipped into the past, but life and death are so strange that imagination falters even before one starts thinking about them, and it's only in those curious moments between two sleeps in the middle of the night that the mere fact makes its impact. Well, God bless them wherever they are. The sidaleia has disappeared from the gate at 13 M.T. It begins to be difficult to think oneself back into that strange time. How I wish the past didn't swallow up our lives!"*

In the summer of 1951 Alison had bought the two upper floors of a converted house not far from Mayfield Terrace – 11 Brights Crescent. A long flight of stairs from the front hall led to the first floor with three rooms and a kitchen and bathroom, all good rooms, and above, up another considerable flight, was the spare room, pleasant and remote, like Alison's own bedroom in Aberdeen. David slept there whenever meetings brought him to Edinburgh, and many of Alison's friends enjoyed that room while she lived at Brights Crescent. Even now it seems to offer its simple, assuring hospitality as though nothing were necessary but the fixing of dates and the buying of railway tickets to establish the old sequence of reunion and delight.

The large, light sitting-room on the first floor had a bow-window facing south-west and in the road outside there grew a service tree (not the true service tree, *Sorbus domestica*, but the whitebeam, *Sorbus aria*) which gave her great pleasure and solaced her for having only a small area of back garden, and not the strength to cultivate even that, in spite of the "almost religious pleasure" it gave her to grow flowers. She no longer found it possible to keep a cat, another very sad deprivation, for she loved cats as much as she detested birds unless *cooked*.

* Alison to David from Edinburgh, 27 July 1952

Although this new home was purchased in 1951, it took Alison almost a year to make it habitable and accomplish her flitting, but in the end of June 1952 she could postpone no longer the unpacking of all the cases that had been in store since Mayfield Terrace was let and Granby Road sold. The avalanche began to rumble down upon her, china, linen, books – the libraries of her parents and grandparents, great-uncles, uncles and aunts, chiefly philosophical and theological, "an exhausting mix-up of things," all to be unpacked and sorted and each item conveyed to an appropriate lodge. The sofa was soon piled high with books, but she went through them *beating* and *dusting* – she so sensitive to dust – and put what she herself wished to keep on the shelves of the handsome bookcase that filled the east wall of her living-room. Thirteen cases were repacked for the saleroom (she had some help with this), three sent at once to David in Aberdeen, and seven kept for him to examine later, while two more went up to the attics. It was all done with great care and patience. She posted me an obscure little book, her uncle Willie's copy of the Reverend H. M. Neville's *Under a Border Tower*, guessing correctly that only I in her circle, or possibly in the whole country, would wish to read and possess it. Discriminate giving like that is more than a virtue, it is a grace. At the completion of this Herculean task, Alison escaped for a short holiday to Aberdeen, and then for a day to Biggar, where I was visiting my mother, now 87. She described her in a letter to David. "Tall, very thin, a bit shaky, but her conversation as of old, rich and racy. William, Lyn's son aged twelve and as fair and beautiful as an angel, sat exchanging quick amused glances with me as his grandmother flowed on.* Our entertainment in the afternoon (it was not one of the superb days but grey and windy) was kite-flying on the golf-course. I feel this a pastime I cd. take up with pleasure. All one's kite-flying experiences of childhood were so frustrating – or almost all. But William's kite was an R.A.F. one like a little orange canvas box and it went sailing up into the wind. He let me hold it, and then bring it down gradually, only pulling it in when the wind allowed one

---

* It was on this occasion that William said: "I ought to have brought my tortoise with me – Grannie would have been *enchanted* with him."

and one felt the string slacken. It was a lovely exhilarating occupation."

In her eighty-ninth year my mother came to live with us at Cross Farm, for she had latterly grown very blind and very deaf. When Alison visited us in 1954 she was happy to find how well she could push her way through to the unchanged person – thanks to the enunciation that had been so helpful talking to the deaf old peers on the Hellenic cruise. She showed her the ruby and diamond ring which she had inherited from her Aunt Kirsty, pleased that its sparkle and colour could be seen, and charmed by my mother's comment, "But Alison, anything attached to my frame drives me mad." (The reason perhaps for her losing so many wedding rings in one married life.) "It was marvellous to see your *dear* mother, and to feel she was well within reach, though by always forgetting and raising my voice I must have constantly reminded her of breaking glass or made her feel as if chewing cinders" – my mother's description of her sensations when people shouted to make her hear. My mother rarely spoke without using language which was Biblical in its strength and imagery. I had taken her about this time to a specialist in Cambridge and as we sat in his delightful drawing-room waiting for some eye-drops to take effect, she took my hand and said pensively – "Little did I think when I cared for you long ago as a baby thing, that I was feathering my latter days." I am sure that to her this seemed just an ordinary way of talking.

A LISON RESIGNED from the Civil Service in 1951 and was free in February 1952 to go to Somerset and spend a few more months on the Clark family records and letters, and again have the pleasure of being with Roger and Sarah Clark. On the way back in May, she paid a series of visits, staying with the Baileys in Oxford and then with us in Manchester* before going on to a reunion at the Mount in York. I had recently bought an electric mixing machine called a chef, which Alison examined with much interest, as becoming her own cook was now her fate. "Lyn, it is NOT a chef, it is simply a kitchen-maid with no wits and very strong arms." When she was saying good-bye, she congratulated me on never having been incommoded by her presence in the kitchen. "Most of my friends send me out." "My dear Alison, haven't you noticed how the meals were served later and later every day? It takes me three times as long to do the simplest thing, I'm so fascinated by what you're saying. You put me out too much for me to know what's happening on the stove at all."

In June she actually began to live at Brights Crescent and cooked kippers for her first lunch there, the charwoman showing her how. Three days later she had progressed to stew with carrots, turnips and potatoes – "not bad but not very good" – and in a few months she was recording some triumphs, and had decided that there was not on the whole much mystery about eating well.

"I should love you to see my flat, it has one very nice room, my living-room, large high-ceilinged with a big bow window facing south – walls pale pale mushroom with a cream coloured spot. Dark mushroom fitted carpet, paint cream. Very large glass-fronted bookcase in 3 parts faces the window (the kind you

* Where we had a house from 1946–53; Cross Farm was let

114

see in v. good lawyers' offices), Chesterfield sofa, 2 lug armchairs (one in window). Old round table and regency chairs in window. Corner cupboard w. grt. grandmother's Crown Derby. Grt. grt. grandfather's writing bureau and country Chippendale chairs. My own mother's bureau-bookcase in Dutch marquetry. No pictures. I put in a new fireplace with Sofono fire which never goes out. Lyn it is rather nice. I feel as if my life were beginning again."*

In the autumn of 1952 Robert Hurd drew her back into the Saltire Society, as its first organizing secretary. This was a solution which some of her friends deplored, considering the Saltire too small a field for her gifts. But Alison so thoroughly distrusted movements, bodies, public endeavours, that she liked the smallness of the Saltire, and its dependence on a few inspired and devoted people, Robert, Agnes, John Oliver,† Sir John MacEwen, John and Elizabeth Noble, Isobel Dunlop. She was employed on a part-time basis which suited her very well. She could sleep late after a disturbed night, and indeed on one occasion slept so late and soundly that a prentice lad coming to work in the flat rang Mrs Palmer's bell on the ground floor, to ask hopefully if Miss Cairns might be dead. She used to make her way to her office in the Lawnmarket between ten and eleven, but often stayed until an hour that more than compensated for this. Gladstone's Land, the handsome sixteenth century house, which had been the Saltire headquarters since the middle of the war, contains two large and beautiful reception rooms, much in use at the time of the Edinburgh Festival, but Alison's office at the back was small and stuffy, cold and dark. Sir John MacEwen, president of the society, worried silently to see her there. He felt it must be bad. "Not that she would not scout any such suggestion with scorn. For a more wholly unselfish person I never knew; herself did not interest her at all." That was the impression she gave, quite unintentionally, by preferring in the main to talk about what she reckoned were

---

* Alison to Lyn from Edinburgh, 22 November 1952

† John Oliver died suddenly towards the end of March 1957. It was a personal grief to Alison and many others, and a great loss to the Saltire Society. She was happy that he had a beautiful and "very Christian" funeral service, such as her father would have approved.

more interesting and amusing subjects. But she was of course intensely interested in herself, and could fight with passion for the consideration that was her due. It was Alison who said to Witold *But I also am a person.*

Edinburgh houses were never built to be heated by gas or electric fires, which are poor substitutes for wood or coal burning in every grate and filling with flame and smoke and hot air the great core of chimneys from which the warmth penetrated the massive stone walls, so that these were never cold at any time of the year. The burghers of earlier centuries never suffered as Alison and her friends did after the domestic revolution of the thirties. "Such a gentle revolution," she called it; such a lethal revolution, if we knew half the story. Alison contrived to keep her sitting-room comfortable with the combination of an open coal fire and electric radiators, but her flat as a whole was never warm in winter, and the bathroom – the place where it so easy to catch a chill in any case – was perishing. "Very miz. with cold" Alison often scribbled in her diary, and she would call in her doctor, Robin Thin, who ordered a couple of days in bed and put her on penicillin to bring down her temperature.

Some months after she had moved into Brights Crescent she was joined by Janet Smith, the Shetland housekeeper who had been with the aunts at Granby Road. Janet cleaned the flat and cooked the midday meal, and ministered to Alison in many unsolicited ways – she was "my good Janet, my kind Janet," and when Alison returned late at night from a meeting, perhaps in Glasgow, she used to find the fire blazing and a bowl of porridge sitting on the hob.

"The difference having this admirable woman makes! My home is civilised and comfortable, the aluminium saucepans shine like silver, the dusters are always so clean I can hardly bring myself to use them. She has character and humour but HATES the Pope, but she is so adaptable, cheerful and kindly in every way that I imagine this fanatical passion is the safety valve for all her negative and aggressive instincts and I have stopped protesting or attempting to modify her notions."

Alison believed now that she had left convalescence behind, and ought to be able to live a normal life, and when she was disappointed, lost patience with herself, snapping out in her diary "Can this tiredness be neurotic?" unaware how the effort of breathing and the fits of coughing lowered her. The fifth column in her illness was her inability to recognize weakness or fatigue as part of the illness. But the damaged lungs sampled every change in the atmosphere with a quickness not without reward. Besides the raw and the damp and the foul air, and the air so cold that it made her ill, there was pure, fine, sweet air, which no one ever relished more; the wind off the hills and the freshness rising from the garden. "Stand and scream" parties were out. She did breathing exercises, dieted to reduce her weight so that she had less to carry up that punishing flight of stairs to her flat, and when she went shopping for new clothes, she took with her a pocket scale to weigh each purchase. But whatever she did, it was without fuss, without harping, and she enjoyed what she was able to do with an ardour such as one rarely meets in the whole and well.

"Last Friday I drove up to Ardkinglas (Loch Fyne) in heavy rain – I thought of Elis. and the windscreen being like a fish-monger's window. At Arrochar I could hardly see through it. I had a wonderful reception from the Nobles. Saturday was better weather, and Sunday and Monday glorious. I spent much time in the walled garden, picking black currants and wild straw-berries, and, fascinating occupation, snapping the dead heads off azaleas – the delightful thing about this is that long after the azaleas have stopped flowering, the bushes give off their delicious scent. The garden has a very high wall, beyond that, great forest trees, oaks that have grown to prodigious size, wonderful beeches and limes, and then rising beyond them, the high green steep peaks of the mountains, often in bright sunlight. My head kept singing over and over 'Yet not the less, Cease I to wander where the Muses haunt, Clear spring and shady grove and sunny hill.'* I always think that last adjective so unexpected and beautiful. We fed on chicken, freshly caught salmon, wild strawberries and cream. I came back on Monday afternoon, much the better."†

* *Paradise Lost*, Book iii, lines 26–28
† Alison to David from Edinburgh, 3 July 1957

The first winter at the Saltire Society, she found no energy to spare after the day's work. "There are just no margins. . . . But I am very well, not so burdened really as this sounds, not so much burdened perhaps as nervous and anxious. An illness like mine makes one lose one's physical self-confidence," which in her case had for many years never faltered. My mother recommended the Howard Loaf, Bemax and Haliver Capsules, and Alison wrote to tell her that she was following all her precepts – so that my mother should know the rare joy of having a convert. In the middle of the second winter she wrote a little more hopefully. "At last I am beginning to feel something of my old vigour. I don't tire so quickly, and I don't get *so* tired and I recover more easily from fatigue. I don't suppose I shall ever walk for pleasure again – you know, feeling the delight of it in one's backbone and one's thighs, but I get about, and I still have my little car without which I couldn't manage."

To have a car and drive herself about almost amounted to owning a spare lung. She made it a cloister on wheels, a sheltered place where she took a turn with friends whom she encountered in the steep and wind-swept streets of Edinburgh. She stopped on the Mound one day when she saw George MacLeod and Ralph Morton battling up it together. "George squeezed himself into the back seat with great difficulty (big man in big ulster) uttering instead of grunts, *yells*, so that everyone turned to see what was happening. I laughed and laughed and said 'The Moderator enters my car.' When the moment came to decant them he extricated himself with the same uproar. About thirty years rolled away, for the parent and one of my uncles had the same obliviousness to what might be said or thought, and indeed used to take a kind of fiendish pleasure in embarrassing us, exclaiming 'You're so PROPER.' "*

"Dear Mrs de Glehn (who used to live in C.bridge, did you know her) telephoned last Saturday and asked me to lunch with her at Moray Place to meet Frances Cornford whom of course I had known by name for a very long time. She is now a very intense but agreeable lady of 70. I liked her much and we wasted no time in polite gabble. She had never been in Scotland

* Alison to Lyn from Edinburgh, 4 November 1956

before. Mrs de Glehn had driven her out in the morning and I took them both out in my car in the afternoon, out to Swanston and then just cruising about the streets. Mrs C. said it all felt so *foreign* and yet so familiar from the Scott and Stevenson she had passionately read as a girl."*

One of the features of her letters became the motion pictures she gave of Edinburgh, seen hazardously from the driving wheel. She was with a small party of friends at the Roxburghe one summer evening, but left after the conversation had turned into "an immense argument of a philosophical religious nature all abt. God and Relationship and what Plato meant by knowledge."

"The houses on the Mound reflected a wonderful green light from the north while the valley of Princes St lay in shadow and as we plunged down Hanover St fr. George St in my car, this illuminated ridge sank quickly below the dusky mass of the R.S.A. and Nat. Gallery buildings. One of those many summer evenings that one will remember after years." Or it might be "one of those moments when one knows one couldn't live anywhere but in Edinburgh."

"I gave Phoebe MacKeller dinner at the International Club and we came into Princes Street about nine o'clock. The sun was down and there was a gentle grey bloom on the castle and its ridge. A strong scent of wallflower came up from the yellow banks of it in Princes Street Gardens and at that moment the bell ringers in St Cuthbert's Church broke out into chimes." And with the mention of those chimes there comes to me a succession of pictures, all familiar to Alison too: Aidan dying propped against the west wall of Bamburgh Church, and his spirit appearing that night to a shepherd boy on the Lammermoors, the boy Cuthbert who became a monk at Coldingham Priory, near Ayton – its collegiate church, Dunglass! – and stood in the sea at night to pray, and played with the otters on the beach when dawn came.

---

* Alison to Lyn from Edinburgh, 7 October 1956

WHEN ALISON fell ill in 1948, Robert Hurd had proved himself a very stout friend and his delightful letters enlivened her months in hospital. Her first appearance in Edinburgh when she recovered was at the Robert Louis Stevenson Centenary Celebrations as Robert's guest. (She sat between Compton Mackenzie and Moray McLaren at dinner and warmed to Moray but not to Compton Mackenzie.) And now that she was settled at Brights Crescent Robert's frequent yet casual visits, either as her architect or her boss, or just as a very old and good friend, were the sap of life to Alison. His unreliability still vexed her, but when he did arrive, then he stayed; probably for hours beyond his intention or her expectation. But Alison, so Robert told me, "sometimes flared up – you know the way she did" (but that I did not) and he used to check her by threatening to go! For Alison this was a novel and disconcerting situation; Robert did not frighten her and it was hard to imagine that she frightened him. Yet for a vulnerable creature like Robert, it was alarming to cross swords with a woman as nearly invulnerable as Alison, accustomed to truth and magnanimity "in the widest sense of the word." One day when Robert, emotionally cornered, flourished a dummy martyr to fend her off, she stabbed the sawdust without mercy, and was never forgiven. "I should never have said it," but it was said, and she lost with the flash of a single penetrating comment, the most valued friend of those post-war years.

"At our age, how easy to make acquaintances, how difficult friends. One becomes at once more lenient and more exacting, more lenient to the acquaintances, more exacting in deciding whom one really does want to see a lot of." "O dear," she wrote later, "there is so much to hear and to say. I do miss my buddies, in Edinburgh. Robert used to be a male buddy till he dropped me. I was so interested to hear your impression of him. He has great charm, he can put himself across, and he has too the solidity of which you speak – he is full of conflicting qualities, complex and inconsistent.

"The trouble is that I am gregarious. I like company, I need company – and the unmarried woman has to exert herself to find it. This is something I had never anticipated. I always thought of myself with dozens of friends easy of access, and never gave one thought to marriage for a home or for company. I don't think I should miss them now if I were free and able to run about. But being now of a more or less dévote turn of mind, I take this present condition as *meant*, and indeed from the point of view of one's inner life there are advantages – one is less 'Distracted from distraction by distraction.' "*

When Billy Graham came to Edinburgh in 1955 Alison regarded his campaign with a good deal of favour, more than I expected her to feel. "What is it Lyn that he has – all that he says one has heard 10,000 times, but what is the quality, passion, conviction, sincerity, but some *plus* in addition to all this that makes the impact. Last night with Tertia† I went to one of the relayed services at St George's, but there I must say one felt some element almost of threat, of more pressure certainly in the sermon and the urgent, prolonged and persistent invitation to people to come forward. Most of those who came forward in the church were little young things, whom one felt should not have been subjected to such pressure. But I should say that the positive gain infinitely outweighs the disadvantages."§

If her earlier step from without to within the church had been made with any reservations, these were now withdrawn. "David, I realize there is no alternative to belief." The over-familiarity of the New Testament troubled her, and she had never been able to read St John's Gospel, but after I had suggested Father Ronnie Knox's translation, she wrote that she was now reading it with intense interest, not pained by the language as in other

* Alison to Lyn from Edinburgh, 20 April 1953
† Tertia Liebenthal, for many years a close friend of Alison's and well known in Edinburgh musical circles as the organizer of the lunch-time concerts
§ Alison to Lyn from Edinburgh, 24 April 1955

modern translations. She recommended the writings of Simone Weil to me. "So strange – I expect you know about her, a French Jewess who died young in this country during the war. One is fascinated and repelled – I think I should have been repelled personally by her, and yet as one reads there comes the queer sensation of a new dimension." Alison and I had now reached a point where all the topics that had been taboo in our youth came naturally into our conversation and letters; for instance, the acceptability of the resurrection of Jesus Christ, but the inacceptability of his ascension, and then the awkwardness of believing the one miracle and not the other. Where did the risen master go?

Sex however she discussed rarely with me, possibly deeming it "more impressive as lived than as propounded," and on the rare occasion with some impatience, brushing it aside – "O those German psychiatrists – always wanting people to hop into bed together." She was reluctant to ask questions in case a situation by discussion might harden at the edges, as she put it. But at the offer of confidence immediately all her attention and sympathy came into play, and with those who were suffering her imagination never failed. When she appears now in my dreams, the quality by which I know her as Alison is attentiveness, a divine readiness to listen and be informed.

Her social life now consisted mainly of quiet and pleasant chat, when she dropped in on Agnes and Jean Mackenzie on her way back from Gladstone's Land, or went down to Louie Palmer in the flat below at Brights Crescent, or round to the Macmurrays, or made her regular calls on Aunt Barbara and Uncle Jo, and her old cousin Bertha, who figures frequently in the diaries. "To see Cos Bertha so v. sweet, amusing, kind, tho' she doesn't know what will become of her. Memory gone, ill, not much money." She was adored by these friends, by all her friends, and Jean Mackenzie who could survive the death of her beloved sister, could not survive Alison's.

In 1953 Max arranged to spend six months' sabbatical leave at Cambridge, living in St John's College, so I was endeavouring to let our house in Manchester and move back into part of Cross Farm. "I hope," wrote Alison on 8 March 1953, "all your plans worked out as you described them and that you and William are enjoying the Spring at Comberton and will write soon and tell me so. I have quite a sense of discomfort in that when I last heard of you, you were all in this complicated state of transition and I have a sort of feeling that you are still flapping about in Limbo and should like to hear that you have come to rest." As it happened our first month had been spoilt by influenza, and although none of us had been seriously ill, the mere mention of it, as an excuse for my silence, brought a letter of sympathy back. "You poor things what a horrible time you had in the early spring with illness and flitting. Health is the first thing, and when one has it one thinks nothing of it. Just this last week I have begun to feel more vigorous and so I am hopeful that the easy exhaustion into which I fell, really is a phase."*

When David and Rosemary adopted their first child, she wrote most happily of this new enlargement of their life and hers. She discovered herself in aunthood – like Jane Austen – and indeed she was remarkably like her, "a woman of great vitality, of generous impulses, of a large-hearted charity; gifted in a pre-eminent degree, with that power of intuitive sympathy in which women excel."†

"I went up to see Elisabeth Mary Cairns in Aberdeen at Easter, a darling creature with great eyes and a dimple in one cheek only. Rosemary is enchanted and has ceased to mourn. David with her little paws clasping his forefingers makes her conduct Toreador." Rosemary's leap into motherhood was not Alison's idea of heaven at all. "Can't you imagine it? – free as air one day and laid by the heels the next – no preparatory nine months to get one's ideas adjusted." But as on other occasions her dismay at the business and bother of child-rearing (increased perhaps by early memories of being a business and a bother herself) was swept aside by fascination in the personality of the child. Here is Elisabeth in the summer of 1954, "at that most trying stage of handling coal, drinking ink, and throwing whatever will make a splash into the lavatory. She came into my room every morning, put on my little grey hat, blue leather

---

* Alison to Lyn from Edinburgh, 20 April 1953
† *Jane Austen, Facts and Problems* by R. W. Chapman. Oxford. p. 102

gloves and seized my handbag, then drawing off right glove extended right hand with 'Ah do you do?' To think that anyone who has been in this world for 19 months should so seize on the panoply of social life quite frightened me." On this visit to Aberdeen, "We had," she wrote, "beautiful runs up Deeside and Donside, the country then being at a stage of early summer with deep pink wild roses, honeysuckle and buttercups waving at the roadsides, and all the trees still in their full, if not their first, green freshness. I had forgotten how the ash tree prevailed in the north and how beautiful a tree it is, preserving its own form, never losing itself in foliage. We had a good deal of sun and days of luminous greyness, beautiful when we got up on the ridge between Dee and Don with a great expanse of country and of sky around us." Lucy Jack, the widow of Professor A. A. Jack, had died that year in Aberdeen, gentled through her widowhood by her faithful staff and by Flora Burley and other former students of her husband's. "I took Flora Burley to lunch at Watt and Grant, and she told me about Mrs Jack. Flora went to see her every week. She had two or three such visitors, each of whom she asked to do different kinds of shopping for her. Flora did books and book-presents. To another was entrusted *combinations*. When Professor Jack died, no arrangements had been made for his funeral which was taken by the Rev. Mr Lawrence, minister of Rubislaw Parish Church (and a very nice quiet circumspect man) but of course it was a Christian burial, and the Jacks were not Church Christians, so Mrs Jack made all the plans for her own dismissal – certain friends to be invited, taxis to be sent for them to accompany her to the Crematorium. The coffin was carried up, set down beneath the pall and sank from sight, and the dozen or so friends who had filed in to the rows of chairs, then quietly filed out. 'It was like seeing someone off,' said Flora.

"One Sunday night we went out to service and supper at Haddo where David and June Gordon now live (the next Marquis and Marchioness of Abdn but one) with their 4 adopted children. Because of June Gordon's choir and the fact that for their big performances they bring up the best singers and instrumentalists from London, the place has become a great musical and social centre for the North East. It is an immense and splendid house (William Adam) full of treasures, with a state diningroom and so on, and the only resident staff are the children's nanny and undernurse. A series of daily women keep it clean and June Gordon does all the cooking herself – a fantastic social transformation and yet on the other hand what a gentle revolution it has been."*

A couple of years later after John had joined Elisabeth and the Cairns family were on holiday at Kirkwall: "The children are adorable, but how do parents survive that 2-year old stage when no toy has the attraction of a box of knives, when every cupboard must be investigated? John and Elisabeth looked enchanting rushing round the garden with Mrs Rose's best tea cosies (specially quilted by the W.R.I.) on their heads, rattling a box containing all the most precious parts of the meat mincer." That was her first visit to Orkney – in 1956 – and Alison wrote to me that she was glad to have seen the islands at last to know the setting of Edwin Muir's autobiography, and for the better appreciation of many of his poems. "He is one of the very few people I know whom one feels to be of perfect integrity 'whose hands are clean whose heart is pure, and unto Vanity who hath not lifted up his soul.' "

Also among the very few were the Juillards, to see whom and Bess she made a special visit to Geneva – "a place for which I have an inexpressible affection" – in the summer of 1955. It was her first holiday abroad since before the war, and she was very happy enjoying "the food, the smells, the lake, the sun, the music." "I had no sense of melancholy as for 'temps perdu.' And in the 26 years that have passed since I first knew the Juillards – 24 since I left Geneva, I found that we had become intimate friends – they could tell me things and I, them, that would never have been said at the point where our friendship stopped in 1931, to be carried on after by no more than yearly letters."

* Alison to Lyn from Edinburgh, 5 September 1954

ARLY in 1955 I had news to give Alison of my mother, whose ninetieth birthday was drawing very near. She had suffered a coronary thrombosis, but rallied after some hours, and regarded her three daughters gathered round her bed. "How are the mighty fallen!" she exclaimed ruefully. "I hoped so much it would never come to this." "But think how nice for us to be able to do something for *you* at last – we'll remember it all our lives." "Ah, you are lovely, lovely," and she folded her arms across her breast as if to embrace us all. Until the sleep of her last night carried her over into the brief coma from which she did not wake, she was just as she had always been, so mindful and naive and humorous; grateful for the short respite to give us her last words of love and assurance, and facing eternity with perfect confidence.

"I was so glad to hear how easily your mother got away – wonderful for you and for her. Yes that strange forgetting – I remember it particularly with Aunt Jessie, several things happened in connection with her funeral arrangements that really were very funny and that would have particularly appealed to her type of humour and I kept thinking O I must tell Aunt J. this. They are still so much with us, just after they go, and then there comes a period when one feels that one's conception of them is for the first time adequate. You are standing back from the mountain and seeing it as a whole. When they are people like your parents and mine it is a very consoling vision. Quite apart from one's sorrow and sense of loss, the death of an old person, full of years and goodness and faith, is a wonderful experience to live through. When I think of your mother now, it is always at Westfield Terrace that I see her, and I can hear the very tones of her voice when she says your names as if the very speaking of them gave her pleasure."*

* Alison to Lyn from Edinburgh, 1 February 1955

"I would like so much to have a letter from you," she wrote on February 20. "This is a spontaneous cry of affection and friendship bursting forth in spite of my guilty conscience that your long and absorbing letter to me, written in mid-October, has gone unanswered until now – so that you could if you wished and without self-reproach remain silent until June. But I hope you won't. You must miss your mother a great deal. Do you feel too, as I did, that a great piece of your own life has fallen away – the early instinctive part. I went I remember in September 1946 to stay near Foulden, at Nunlands, and the familiarity of all that Border country of my earliest memories was extraordinarily dear and comforting. It was a pilgrimage like yours to Berwick of last June. Your mother's death must have made a big difference to your everyday life too. Lovely for you Lyn, to think of what you were able to do for her this last year and that you were able to send her on her way, as it were warmed and cheered.

"14 March 1955. This fragment of three weeks ago will go in to show you that you had been in my thoughts, and so to speak at the point of my pen, when your long letter of Feb 25th came in. O Lyn yes. I do so agree with you; one has a need to brood over events of such magnitude and not to hurry them into the background of one's consciousness through the hustle of daily life, or through fear of being overwhelmed by them. It takes a great effort of realisation to assimilate the fact of death and that the person one loves *has disappeared*. I can't think that the life of the spirit hereafter has as little resemblance as you think to anything we know or imagine, there must be some identity of personality which will be dear and familiar – that is if there is any personal immortality. And I just cannot think that the personality, so strong, so complex, the fruit of so much experience, disintegrates and disappears with death, it is too *unlikely*. We go through most of our lives with a kind of veiled conception of the people we love, in their essence they are revealed to us only intermittently and I think sometimes we only begin to apprehend them, three dimensionally as it were, after death. Is this possibly the beginning of a new knowledge or a new way of knowing that will develop later? Who can say. But sometimes it feels like that.

127

I could see her so clearly as you wrote of seeing her through the window, old and frail. O Lyn isn't human life infinitely pitiful when it's looked at from outside and isn't it a queer paradox that when we turn the eye of pity on ourselves, we become so contemptible and displeasing to others. Why? and to indulge in self-pity really is as fatal as to drink poison. Life looks like pathos and tragedy but mercifully it feels more like a battle."*

I do not remember what I had said about survival after death – unless it was that when one outgrew the myth of the spirit housed in the body and accepted the person as an entity so inwoven that (for example) a philosopher without toes cannot prevent his toelessness affecting his philosophy, then it was hard to conceive what recognition of the self, or the other-than-self might still exist after death. But what is hard to conceive is not by that token impossible. We may have no argument and yet take a stand with the old woman who silenced Darwin's father. "Doctor, I know sugar is sweet, and I know that my redeemer liveth."

On the pilgrimage to Berwick which Alison mentioned, she had joined me, and we stayed two nights at the Red Lion at Ayton, and visited many scenes of our early memories. I was astonished to find so little changed in the course of half a century and after two world wars, and happy to refresh my memories for a book I was writing about my parents and my childhood. But when we came to Foulden Alison gave a cry of distress. All the beech trees that had been the chief glory of the place had been felled, and judging by the raw stumps, recently too. It had been done to "let in the light." The old shepherd, Paterson, was still living in one of the farm cottages, and he and his wife welcomed Alison as kith and kin, but nothing could console her. The second morning of our holiday she slept through the breakfast gong and alarmed me by not answering my knock on her bedroom door. Her ears were plugged with wax to shut out disturbing sounds. For a long time now she had suffered from insomnia and rarely slept through the night at the best of times, but woke to cough, take a soothing drink, and read. Then hoping to sleep on in the morning, she plugged her ears and

* Alison to Lyn from Edinburgh, 14 March 1955

128

wrapped a silk scarf over her eyes to keep out the light – a device recommended to her by Reinhold Niebuhr. That second day we lay in the sun on the slope of Gallows Law, where a track goes off to an earthwork, and ate our picnic lunch. Alison talked of Robert Hurd and his defection which still grieved her, but the sunshine lay softly on Cheviot, just as we had both seen it as children, just as Alison's mother described it in the letter from the shepherd's cottage at Rawburn writing to "Mr David." We visited many of Alison's family graves – not Bonkyl, although we passed very near it – but those of the Craws at Foulden and of the Cairns at Cockburnspath and then the Browns at Haddington. I had so little anticipation of my curiosity in days to come that I was no more than politely attentive while Alison hunted out the stones commemorating so many of the family from the Dunglass cottage.

From the time of this pilgrimage I was never free of apprehension for Alison, and I remember no darker moment than when it first seemed probable that I should survive her, possibly by many years – *ne sachant avec qui rire finement.* If word reached me that she was ill, I used to ring up from Cambridge, and soon she developed the habit of ringing me back immediately for another six minutes or so. "How lovely to have you come breaking into my convalescent evening last Tuesday. After we had stopped talking I had an impulse to go on, and looked you up in my address book I have had since my early twenties – almost all my life in it, but *not* Lyn. Well it must just be that like Lochton or 20 Braidburn Crescent, she has been too familiar ever to be written down. So I got Telephone Directory Enquiries. They could find no trace of you. They rang off and the best part of an hour later telephoned with your number. By that time it was getting on for ten o'clock. You might have been in bed, you might have been asleep. I thought I'll make it a letter. When I woke later in the middle of the night, I realised I had been looking you up in my address book under I! Under N there were six entries for you including your telephone number, I now find.

"Lyn 2 things operate against one's writing to one's oldest dearest and most intimate friends, the first is a wish to write a letter that says something and does not only chit-chat. The second is that they are so much part of one's consciousness, so often in and out of one's thoughts, that one does not realise how long it it since there has been an exchange in the outside world of letters and news."*

I was often myself under the impression that I had written an account of current events at Cross Farm, and even received her comments, only to discover that it was all one of these imaginary conversations; while some of the most memorable words in her letters became remembered as spoken not written when I reflected on them. In such ways factual life and its barriers start breaking up long before life comes to an end.

I had been working by fits and starts since 1948 on the story of my childhood in Berwick-upon-Tweed and memories of my parents and grandparents. The manuscript vanished for a couple of years and survived as some neglected infants do through an inborn obstinacy. In 1956, when it was finished, my first completed book for twenty-four years, I sent it to Faber and Faber – starting from the beginning all over again, an unknown writer again, without the trump card of youth which had proved so advantageous thirty years earlier. As I waited week after week for Faber's decision, I fell quite silent – as far as letters went – turned in on my suspense, until the day that I was able to write and tell Alison that it was accepted. She replied with what she called a *Shriek of Joy* – "Wonderful, how lovely. I am so *pleased*. To go right in at the top like this. You must be overflowing with joy and exultation. I can hardly wait to see it – how long will it take to come out? in time for Christmas?" Alas, my exultation had taken the form of a temperature and a headache, and her pleasure all through, being selfless and consistent, was greater than mine. However when she came to stay with me a couple of months later and read the manuscript we both felt the same satisfaction that Alison had felt thirty years earlier reading Francis' *Conte de Six Semaines*. Now we could see a pattern where before was confusion. A part of life known to us both had been pulled from beneath all the irrelevant, universal litter, the cosmic dust that desecrates even the highest snowfields. At this advanced date, how curious to discover –

* Alison to Lyn from Edinburgh, 14 January 1956

when her father and mine were both dead – that we had both as small children consciously confused our fathers on earth with our father in heaven. She wrote on her return to Edinburgh that the book had given our days together a fourth dimension – "It was all so real to me." In her diary for this week I saw long afterwards "To read it is an experience – the quintessence of so much that one remembered. A re-creation." What praise from someone who put nothing higher than the sacrament of history, the securing of the past as meaningful now.

We met again at the end of August 1956 when I made another pilgrimage to the Borders, this time to Rule Water and Jed Water, tributaries of the River Teviot, that noble consort of the Tweed. This was the countryside so well known to my father's father as a boy. Here was the place of his vision, marked for him by a patriarch of a tree, growing on the eastern slopes of Wolfelee, a solitary remnant of the great Jed Forest, spared it could hardly be by accident. Alison joined me on the second day, and I told her how I had already followed the walk taken by my grandfather on the old drove road that runs from the north-west of the hill over into Jed Water, and described the thrilling sense that came to me – almost a vision – of the little lad plodding before me up the road, a hundred and thirty years ahead of me in time, but those years suddenly like the lifting and falling of a capful of wind over the bent. I did not need so many words to describe it to Alison, as we paused in her car at the entrance to the grassy track, and she exclaimed how glad she was "For so often one hopes to feel so, but cannot." She then followed me on a tour of deserted farmhouses and flaking tombstones with a readiness that made me think with shame of my casual mood two years before in Berwickshire. Looking back from Carter Bar we could still see the great ash tree, ten miles away on the slope of the hill, a totem dominating Jed Water from Carter Fell almost to Ferniehirst, and my grandfather's spiritual adventures took second place to the mystery of the solitary tree in the middle of a field of mangold wurzels.* Still

* The ash is not usually long-lived, but in the parish of Ladykirk in Berwickshire an ash was blown down in 1810 which the Duke of Lauderdale had saved from felling in 1666, on account of its unusual size and beauty *then*; so that it must have spanned two centuries, and I reckon that the Wolfelee ash is now as old, if still standing

in a highly impressionable mood, we drove to Jedburgh and visited the Abbey. I wished to find the grave where Simon and Christina Irvine, my great-grandparents, had been buried. The caretaker looked at me with a kind but incredulous smile. "And ye dinna ken whaur?" But I walked without hesitation to the quiet corner where the stone was standing, still legibly marking the place that their seven little orphans visited so often and so sadly.

Alison was amused to receive an advance copy of my book from Ainslie Thin in May 1957 with a covering note to say that he had glanced through it, and thought she might be interested. Aunt Barbara had fallen downstairs and was in bed with bruises and shock – "My dear, I have a *black bustle* behind" – so Alison took her this copy with injunctions not to show it to her visitors yet. "Next time I went out – 'I have been LIVING in this book. I never met Mrs Irvine, but your mother used to tell me about her and now I feel I know her – and my dear' she went on, 'I have told no one, not even Jo, but always popped the book under the bedclothes when he came in.'

"I was in Aberdeen last weekend, it never stopped raining except for about half an hour last Sunday night when I went with David to an ordination service in the east church of St Nicholas. Lyn did you ever realise that in pre-Reformation days St Nicholas (now 2 churches, East and West) must have been a splendid great church? It was a cold bright evening and Gibb's pillared front (called the Façade in Aberdeen postcards) was laced with fresh green beech leaves and there was a big old gean tree in flower among the graves. It was a lovely service with psalms and paraphrases and familiar hymns and reading of the dignified and simple form of ordination now included in the Scottish Book of Order."*

When my book appeared officially, I was delighted to hear how responsible Alison felt for it. "I find myself saying modestly, as if I were yr sister 'O did you like it, I'm so glad.' To George Bruce (who was rapturous about it) I said I thought it was very good, but then it recreated for me so much, I was bound in a way to think it good. 'O but,' said he, 'that book deals in

* Alison to Lyn from Edinburgh, 26 May 1957

universals.' He said that nowadays he hardly read any prose, novels bored him and so did everything else. Your book was quite another matter." Its publication evoked many signs of old friendship in Aberdeen, so we set off to go there together in October 1957. Alison had Saltire Society business in Elgin and Nairn, and we drove up through Perth to Newtonmore, country once very familiar to both of us. The shape and outline of every hill and glen called up confirming pictures from depths of memory that we had both thought far beyond retrieve.

My childhood's obsession with the huge walls of the Allt Garbhlach had never left me. Gazing at it again from Newtonmore I tried to pierce to the heart of the distant massif of the Cairngorms when the light of the descending sun opened up its dark windings, as baffling as the entrance to the whorls of a shell. Three years later I walked at long last up the little-used path by this most dramatic tributary of the Feshie. Meall Tionaill and Meall Dubhachadh rose up on either side, sheer and discouraging. Like Alison's walk from Spean Bridge to Courrour Halt, it was all longer and rougher than I or my companion expected, and we were obliged to return the way we had come, but first we sat down to rest at the head of a waterfall. It was then that I saw Newtonmore, thirteen or fourteen crow-flying miles away, a sprinkling of little houses among trees, lit by the sun, looking pleasant and inviting and quite incongruous, wedged in the bottom of the great V of the Garbhlach coire. So I knew that I must be sitting where so often my eyes had come to rest nearly a life-time before. Time ceased to be a practical or necessary measure. The limitations of the human body seemed to vanish too. I was young and I was old. The years were a strip of moorland, or even just a beam of light bridging the Feshie and the Tromie and the Spey.

As we left the Cairngorms (Alison and I in 1957) passing little lochs of lambent blue until we came to the wide grey waters of Lochindorb, Alison suddenly drew up at the roadside and stopped the car. She was "épuisée" – to that point where she took the uncommon step of admitting it. After coffee from our flask and some glucose, she revived, and said nothing more about herself as I drove the car for her to Nairn. She put the incident aside, as not of great interest. When Alison did consider any symptom worth discussing she had such a natural easy way of talking that the emotional atmosphere always remained clear. Illness was certainly to be respected, but never held in awe. In November she wrote full of confidence about herself, how well she felt, better than for years. Then in three weeks she was struck down with Asian influenza, and it was more than a week before she knew what was happening. Even in the second week she was too ill to read or see visitors. Janet fed her and soothed her nightmares – "fearful nightmares." "I remember the past fortnight only in patches. Janet has been wonderful nursing me, soothing my nightmares with cups of hot milk at 3 a.m. I cannot believe that all these fevered nights were spent in one bedroom and that my own – I feel as if I had been sleeping in rooms of different character and size all over Edinburgh." A few days afterwards David explained to her that she had had pneumonia. "I certainly never in my life felt so ill even after being carved up. But that is past." Her recovery still took many weeks, but after Christmas she was able to go to Johnstounburn with Tertia Liebenthal to recuperate. They had much sun and "that clear *caller* air that blows off the Lammermuirs, an invigorating not a withering cold." Alison walked every morning very slowly, "but breathing so deeply that it was a buoyant 2 m.p.h." After she returned from Johnstounburn, the weather began to change. It grew daily colder with snatches of premonitory hail, until the snow came, driving in from the east all one Saturday. Alison's car was out of order and she staggered through the blizzard on foot for her weekend's supplies, and then resigned herself to many hours of domesticity alone. She cleared her chest of drawers; washing, ironing, mending; and closed the day "V. satisfied with progress." On the Sunday she woke to deep snow and soon the blizzard set in again, and so she carried on, unhurried and absorbed, from hour to hour, until late in the evening she came to a box of old letters, long undisturbed, dating from school and college days and from the lean years at Aberdeen, some from people who had loved her, other treasured notes from those whose love she might have welcomed. The lost voices sounded with an unearthly clarity in that deep snowbound retreat, sealed off from every human distraction. "All my past rose before me and I watched where my life had gone to." It hurt to see so strange a revelation vanish, but how could she write the story now? It was too late.

The sense of youth as almost a former life had come to stay. She asked me whether I still had "a faint anticipatory thrill" about the future in general, and if I had lost it – as she had – when did it go? She visited Venice with Bess Tapper in September and on the way home stopped for a night in Geneva. The Juillards seemed much older and she walked back to the Hotel Cornavin after lunching with them, through the streets whose very stones were dear to her – "a little sadly, hardly having the heart for it and considering if I shall ever come back. All my life there is in the past." But then Stefa Tixier cheered her, Stefa "as good company as ever, fine, decisive, witty." "Oh dear," she wrote to me, "why do we all live so far away from each other? If we could have the pleasure of being together more often, how lovely it would be, but winter comes and *clamps* us down and shuts us up in our own habitations." But it was there and clamped down that she received the visions that come to the solitary, and saw where her life had gone to, or overheard the surreptitious paces by which the present leaves itself behind. "Half an hour ago, sitting by my fire I heard a faint crackling, rustling sound on the table by the window. I tip-toed to see what it could be. What do you think? In a pot of daffodils one was bursting its sheath – it went on rustling at intervals for over half an hour. Now the trumpet is imperceptibly smoothing itself out."

She and Robert still met for business talks but the long evenings of laughter and discussion were never resumed, nor the weekend outings to North Berwick or Haddington or Dirleton for lunch and tea and walks in the caller air. "One thing struck me re-reading your letter this afternoon à propos of Robert Hurd – you say 'He fears perhaps a vision of himself that he gets in your company' – this may be true, and I have always been aware of the possibility – it was rather borne out when after lunching with me one day he said 'Well this has been very pleasant, you haven't rebuked me.' Judge if I felt a termagant. But honestly Lyn I don't think I ever have rebuked him at these lunches (where we meet to discuss Saltire business) except for being late. Once he kept me waiting 40 minutes. This is a notorious habit of his with everyone, but on that occasion I rebuked him to such effect that he has never since exceeded 10 minutes. Poor Robert, he has his own troubles. But I do not really miss him now. In your letter you go on to say that marriage is often so difficult a relationship because the partners in it tend unintentionally to hold up a mirror to each other. I can well believe this. Isn't it Kübel who says that marriage provides the occasion for relentless confrontation of character through which self-knowledge and what he calls the moment of clarification occurs. I have often wondered how I would have stood up to marriage, not at all I sometimes think now and indeed often feared at the time."*

Edwin and Willa Muir had bought a cottage at Swaffham Prior when they returned from America in 1956 and Alison missed them both from the Edinburgh scene. "Edwin is I think almost the most easy person to communicate with that I ever met – the only other comparable character in that way was – don't laugh – Mr Gandhi. There was the same extraordinary clarity, gentleness and candour. Of course one knew or was told that Mr G. had great depths of wiliness. And Edwin is spiced with a very impish sense of humour." He was in Edinburgh the summer of 1958 and stayed with Alison. "He seemed to me so *fragile*. It was so much more noticeable here than in his quiet village surroundings when I saw him last February. I tried to save him riding in horrible buses and gave him simple food."

Like Alison herself, Edwin had trodden down ill-health for many years, and he was indeed very fragile, but too poor to think of retiring and often obliged to write his articles and reviews when he was suffering, in case younger men stepped into his shoes. Through the autumn of that year I kept Alison posted about the Muirs, giving her the measure of their troubles with Willa's pungent phrase – "This is so bad, it can't be us." But even so, no one was prepared for Edwin's death on 3 January 1959, just a day or two after he had gone into

* Alison to Lyn from Edinburgh, 14 January 1956

Addenbrooke's Hospital for treatment. We all mourned his going. Willa was too ill herself to attend the memorial service at St Giles, and Alison was at special pains to share the experience with her.

"I am not long back from Edwin's memorial service in St Giles and I just want to tell you that it was not unworthy of him. We started with the 23rd psalm – strange that at times like these, well-known words are heard as if for the first time, fresh and full of meaning, and all that pastoral imagery was somehow so appropriate – almost as if it had been Edwin's own. Douglas Young read the 'Remember now thy Creator' passage from Ecclesiastes up to 'and the spirit shall return to God who gave it,' beautifully, sincerely, gravely, and the New Testament passage John XI 1–5 and 19–27 was well read too, I don't know by whom. I hope that Norman MacCaig has written down what he said, and that he will send you a copy. It was very, very good, he spoke of how not only in his poems, but in his reviews, his letters, the slightest thing that Edwin wrote, there was always a perception of truth, some light was cast, and how this was because of his continuous vision of the reality that lies behind appearances and how he let nothing come between himself and it. There was much more of course and he said it well, simply, sincerely and without hesitation. And Tom Fleming read the Transfiguration, again Willa, so simply and sincerely that we listened to *it* and not to him and it was most deeply moving. Then Dr Warr prayed – it was as if Edwin's own quality had for the time being at any rate, called out in all those people a corresponding integrity and clarity and this made it a true and moving memorial occasion.

"The Moray Aisle was full and the people over-flowed into the nave of St Giles. So many of our friends were there, Stanley Cursiter, Willie MacTaggert, Willie Beattie, Sidney Goodsir Smith, Dr Purvis, Lady Rosebery, Mary Ramsay, Helen Cruickshank, Patrick Murray and many many more. You and Gavin are very much in the thoughts of all your friends."*

* Alison to Willa Muir from Edinburgh, 17 January 1959

ALTHOUGH Alison suffered nothing worse than influenza this winter of 1958–9, she found the climb up into the belated Edinburgh spring very hard going. "My heart feels tired which I daresay is nonsense." But her pulse rate was 100. She went in May for a check-up at the hospital, to a new specialist who reminded her of the type of lugubrious church elder she had hated in her youth, "cosy, kind and stupid." When she had made her report he said "in a voice *plangent* with sympathy" – "Yes, gradually deteriorating!" Alison was very angry, and a long pounding day at the typewriter in Gladstone's Land was required to purge the consultation from her system. Then she felt better in every way.

"A high gale is blowing, but the sun is shining," she wrote to David early in June. "When I woke this morning and heard the wind in the trees, I thought

> So some tempestuous morn in early June
> When the year's primal burst of bloom is o'er
> Before the roses and the longest day. . . .

You remember – *Thyrsis* I think – or is it *The Scholar Gypsy?* And suddenly I was back at the Kings Mound and all that it meant to me when I was young – romantic Oxford – and the sense of a traditional and mellow learning and the great kindness and friendship of Gemma and Cyril Bailey. In point of fact I don't suppose the times I stayed with them added up to more than ten days, but how much they counted for in one's experience and in one's picture of the world. Older people often don't realise how much they give to the young."

As a consequence of the rediscovery of Speyside on the short visit of October 1957, I had gone to the Dell in Rothiemurchus with my family the following summer and now Alison and

David and his family went there in July 1959. It was a region dear to the Cairns not only from their own holidays in the twenties, but from much perusing of Elizabeth Grant's *Memoirs of a Highland Lady*, and we were now seeing the last lap of all that simple uncrowded life. In 1959 Alison had preceded David and Rosemary by a few days, and struck a spell of very wet weather. We were staying in Wester Ross, and in sunshine, and persuaded her to drive over and join us. "I set off gladly and left the rain behind me. At Kinlochewe I ran into the magnificent West Highland scenery, the mountains are steeper, barer, rising out of the sea lochs, great presences. The road is single track but with frequent passing places and a good enough surface. About 6.30 I came down to the little cluster of houses where the Newmans were inhabiting a cottage of exquisite comfort, neatness and taste. I can't remember if you ever had a holiday in Wester Ross. I had only been there once for a day, motoring from Strathspey. It still has the loneliness, the unspoiledness that Speyside no longer has. The rivers and burns run full and free, untrammelled by hydro-electric schemes, and no pylons go stalking across the scene. It is incredibly beautiful – both in its distant aspects and its near detail – the little burns and self-sown fir trees and exquisitely scented orchises and the thyme and the cotton grass."* It is a place to which I never return without meeting there the memory of her pleasure, such pleasure as only poets and artists know, sharp as pain, pervasive as the winds of heaven. When she had returned to Rothiemurchus she wrote to me: "I hope this will reach you before you set off. Through driving in a very leisurely way and with two pauses yesterday, I have a feeling of your withdrawnness from the world in that heavenly remote place that makes me think this letter will take days to reach you – this impression rather heightened by seeing the bus broken down on Monday evening. These days have been so lovely. There really was I suppose a day and a half and yet how much we seemed to do and see. In ten years time I shall remember that I spent a *summer* with you there."†

* Alison to Nancy Blackburn from Rothiemurchus, 5 July 1959
† Alison to Lyn from Rothiemurchus, 2 July 1959

At Rothiemurchus, with a dogged use of what strength she had, she went off by herself to find where the Grants had lived and where so many of them now lie. "Did you visit the Doune when you were at Aviemore? It is not anywhere visible from the road and I was determined to find it, so persisting past notices which said 'No road' and 'Private' and other threatening exclamations, I found it at last, at the foot of the boat-shaped hill as Elizabeth Grant described it, but alas, deserted and falling into decay. I don't know when the Grants last lived there. Between the wars I know it was the first home in this country of Kurt Hahn and his school before they moved to Gordonstown, then during the war the army had it and no one has lived there since. I crept round and round the house, peering in at the unshuttered windows. In the library books still stood in wall bookshelves, were piled on tables and stacked on the floor. What had been the dining-room was crammed with furniture, tables, chiffoniers, commodes, all thick in dust. Yet another room was piled with stags' heads with branching antlers, their glassy eyes dim with dust. The drawing-room was empty but as I gazed in, a small ginger and white cat stared at me questioningly and resentfully, as if it were the spirit of Elizabeth Grant. I didn't go in – for one thing I thought I might fall through rotting floor boards, and who would know where I was? – and then it would have seemed somehow an intrusion.

"Another evening and again after some difficulty I found the old parish church and graveyard. The church is roofless, trees are growing in it, one was thrusting a red-berried branch out through a glassless window. All the mown grass of the churchyard had been deposited inside the church and was rotting into a rich mulch. But the churchyard was well-kept and *full* of old friends. Hugh Mackenzie and 'his spouse "Anne Lynch of London"' – you remember the valet and lady's maid who took over the Aviemore Inn, and he became such a drunkard and she was always so loyal and said he was ill or busy; and you remember was criticised by the neighbours for uppishness when she engaged a governess for her children.

"Do you remember the Camerons of the Croft, how warmly she always spoke of him? They had such beautiful carefully chosen texts on their stones – on his: 'For God giveth to a man that is good in his sight wisdom, and knowledge and joy.' Eccles. 2. 26. The Grant burial ground was pretentious and rather tasteless. Bronze plaques were fixed to the wall, the first having the names of all the lairds. Text very pagan: 'One generation cometh another generation passeth away, but the earth remaineth.' Well, perhaps no, perhaps it was a nod to old Shaw lying under his table stone and a recognition that Rothiemurchus itself was more than the possession of a single line." David and Rosemary and Alison were invited to Inverdruie by the Laird. "They told us that the Memoirs had had to be heavily censored and purged before publication and much scandalous material edited away. All this 'Highland Lady' background and interest added so much to the pleasure and richness of our holiday – gave me such a vivid sense of the continuity of human life in that setting, and the poignancy of the generations passing away."*

The wonderful weather which continued through the holiday had followed her to Edinburgh – "such security in day following day of bright sunshine. I feel *quite* different. If only it were always summer." It was still summer in the end of September when she went for a week to stay with Kathleen Morrison-Bell near Bellingham. Very tired after the Edinburgh Festival, she sat all day and every day on the flagged terrace in front of the house, where the sun drew out the scents of the flowers "mignonette, violas, sweet alyssum; tobacco plants and night-scented stock at night. I remember no such scents since I was a child at Foulden. They rose like incense from the flowers, in the hot stillness, no wind or breeze to blow them away." But this week did not set her on her feet, and before the end of October she went into Edinburgh City Hospital for treatment, after which she pronounced her "beams more or less retrick'd" for the early part of the winter in Edinburgh – the early part only. At last admitting that the winds and blizzards had beaten her, she had accepted an invitation from Catherine Hastie to spend most of January and February in Uganda. She wrote to Willa Muir: "I do so hope that the summer has helped you in your health for

* Alison to Lyn from Edinburgh, 3 August 1959

how does one surmount illness and sadness when they come together? Only by hanging on with one's teeth I suppose and when one is in that state there is little incentive to the effort. But there is in you such a strong spring of life that it is bound to run clear and free again. I remember my father once saying that after my mother's death one thought that helped him to bear it was that he was bearing it for her, because if he had died she would be having the unhappiness that was at that time his.

"I had been getting more and more tired and my bronchitis more troublesome, and then a series of events sent me to my specialist and he clapped me into the City Hospital. Willa, it was heaven, after the first three days which were interminable. Bed divinely comfortable, food simple but very good, doctors and nurses kind and clever, and the other women so friendly and interesting. Beds were v. widely spaced so no one's company was imposed on one. The one blot was the unearthly wakening hour of 5 a.m., and the headphones only relayed the Light Programme with Mrs Dale's Diary as the intellectual summit. The rest and warmth cleared my tubes wonderfully. I saw one or two women there frightfully reduced by bronchitis who even in the 2 weeks of my stay had revived as faded flowers do after some hours in a glass of water.

"I like your words for Edwin's stone.* There was a very moving reading of some of his poems one Sunday afternoon at Gladstone's Land in the Music Room (i.e. the room where you and I, you with a red Fez from Cochranes on your head and congratulated by Dr Meikle on your hat from Paris, do you remember, saw Mrs Vere Hodge and her play). [The room] was quite full which would mean about 60 people about 5 o'clock on the middle Sunday afternoon of the Festival 3 Sundays."†

Three weeks later, still feeling the benefit of her treatment, she bought a number of cotton dresses to wear in Uganda, and began to look forward to the change of scene in a way that had grown rare since her operation. She was photographed, looking

---

* The words are from Edwin Muir's poem on Milton. I have already quoted them.
  "His unblinded eyes
  Saw far and near the fields of Paradise"
† Alison to Willa Muir from Edinburgh, 8 November 1959

all her pleasure, but carrying her head with a touch of defiance. Her flight was booked for the twentieth of January, "and for the last few days I have been feeling from 10–15 years younger." This was in a letter that she wrote me in the end of November, and she went on to speak of a mutual friend. "When one is ill with a long serious illness one wants to be with, one craves to be with, people who are well. I think this is instinctive – and also instinctive I think is the desire of old people for the company of the young. This may not be true of people like your parents or my father, but they were after all of the twice-born."

At the beginning of December 1959 the weather turned very cold and Alison was not feeling well when she went for her yellow fever inoculation. A week later she succumbed to gastric influenza, which presently hit Janet also. Louie Palmer, their good friend in the flat below, shopped and cooked for them; but in a day or two, Alison decided that she was on the mend, and got up at intervals to fill hot water bottles for herself and Janet. She had no fever, and dressed and sat in her living-room on Sunday 13 December – hoping to return to work in a couple of days. I rang her up from Cross Farm that evening, and she rang me back, as her custom was, to continue our talk, and showed no weariness in the easy and reassuring chat of those twelve minutes. I think of the meadows on the Berwickshire coast, where the fine clean grass and the wild flowers grow to the very edge of the cliff. In fact she had been sitting staring at the untended fire, unable to summon the energy to take up a lump of coal in the tongs. Her doctor, always deeply solicitous, was calling regularly to see her, but Alison herself was far too accustomed to fighting with her back to the wall to guess that she was losing now. She kept her diary going for four more days. It was full moon on Tuesday 15 and to save herself comment, or the vulgarity of it (Beauty of Nature), she underlined the printed words at the head of the space. Two days later she was still not back at work, but Marian de Glehn came for coffee in the middle of the morning. She had just read my book and wanted to discuss it and Alison was delighted with the visit and talked with such spirit and humour of her childhood and her parents, and my parents – and especially my mother – that Marian felt no anxiety at all. They drove round in Alison's car by Blacket Place to look at the one-storey houses – too handsome to be called bungalows – which Alison coveted for herself and her older friends; no stairs! In the diary: "Marian de Glehn for coffee this morning such a darling." The letters had already come to an end, and with this the diaries end too. Janet was astounded to come on her weeping; Alison made some excuse. It was evident that she could not go north for Christmas to join David and Rosemary and the children at Aldroughty and even her flight to Entebbe might have to be postponed for a week or two. Tertia asked her to Regent Terrace for midday dinner on Christmas Day, and Alison hoped it might do her good to get out of the house. So she dressed and ordered a taxi and endeavoured to eat Tertia's delicious food, but by this time whisky and beaten egg were all she could manage to swallow. Tertia saw her into a taxi to go home and rang in half an hour to make sure that she had gone to bed. But there was no reply. She waited and rang again, by now much perturbed, and finally Alison answered. It had taken her twenty minutes or more to climb the stairs from the front door, resting on each step for breath to climb the next one. Her cousins Stewart and Paula Aitchison, calling on Boxing Day, were alarmed by the dark and far-away look in her eyes and told their mutual cousin Alison Ritchie. When she also came and urged for Alison to go into hospital, it was already too late for her to be moved. At no stage had she appeared as acutely ill as when she had pneumonia two years earlier, yet she had a strange feeling that the drugs (without which she would have choked long before this) were now drying up the stream of life. She ceased to cough. David was warned and left Aldroughty early on the morning of December 30, to be met at the station with the news that Alison had died a few hours earlier – conscious to the end, grateful for the spoonfuls of egg and whisky that Janet fed to her, saying that she felt a little better, and then without a struggle, ceasing to breathe, soul and body parting like friends.

Before night all her friends in Edinburgh had heard the grievous news. Soon it reached Geneva and Bess went to tell the Juillards, who like so many others, had never thought to survive Alison. Stefa, flying from Guatemala to Europe, was met at La Guardia Field by Witold, and they gazed at one another in silence, afraid to speak, and then knew by the silence and the sadness that each had heard already.

LIFE, Alison said, looks like pathos and tragedy, but mercifully it feels more like a battle – and for her the adversary was that angel with whom she wrestled saying "I will not let thee go except thou bless me." This is what I never forget when I think of her. She ruled out self-pity, it had no place in life as she came to see it.

Even if Alison had lived, I cannot imagine her at any age looking back and saying as her father did "I have finished the work I was given to do." And yet I do not think she would have looked back in remorse saying "What have I done?" That whispered reflection in her diary – "I watched where my life had gone to" – so poignant to us, expressed her sense of the obdurate mystery of life. "What asketh man to have? Now with his love, now in the colde grave."

In the train going to Edinburgh to her funeral I slept and saw her flash across my sleeping sight, very young again and a miniature of Alison, dancing and calling out to me "I'm glad you're coming to my funeral – I'm coming too. I've been at Lochton for the weekend." Naturally, for David and Rosemary had gone there to be with the Aitchison cousins. I carried with me a letter she had written three years earlier. "I went to church this morning, a dear old minister, but stuffy rather and he chose such shocking hymns, but for the last we had the 30th Paraphrase, worth the whole of the rest of the service, and worth enduring the rest for. 'Come let us to the Lord our God, With thankful hearts return.' I think it really is beautiful, and not only fond association that makes it seem so, but how heavenly when one has beauty *and* fond associations chiming together." We sang this paraphrase at her funeral service – and it was attended like her father's by a great crowd of friends.* Correctly the first

* Alison was cremated at Warriston Crematorium on 4 January 1960 and her ashes were laid in her mother's grave in Aberdeen

146

verse runs "with contrite hearts return; Our God is gracious, nor will leave the desolate to mourn," but I prefer Alison's misquotation.

When I returned to Rothiemurchus in the summer of 1960, I carried another of her letters, the long elegiac one that she had written the previous year about the Grants, and David and I went to visit the old parish church and graveyard. I expected to see it as Alison had, and hoped to recapture a little of the elevation we had felt together on such explorations, a mood so potent that I could not afterwards recollect quite how we trod the turf or what guided us to our destination. Item by item it was all there, but the life of it was in her description, not in the place itself. This was merely a deserted country graveyard, in a beautiful setting, but not itself beautiful. It was hard to imagine that this dust had not always been dust. What had been so immediate to Alison, and to me when I read her letter, now seemed to have only shadowy significance for anyone. For an hour or two she had given these old friends their resurrection, as she looked out of her own life into theirs, becoming reconciled to what lay imminent for herself in the tranquil contemplation of their past.